I G

CONSCIOUS
LEADERSHIP

Is it Lying Dormant Within You?

1. Endorsed by Dr. Daniel Goleman, Ph.D., author of the New York Times bestseller *Emotional Intelligence*

2. Foreword by John Mattone, World's Top Leadership Coach

IGNITING CONSCIOUS LEADERSHIP

Is it Lying Dormant Within You?

SANDIIP PANNDIT

Life Alchemist & Founder - Soul In Harmony™

*(Globally certified Executive Leadership,
Corporate Mindfulness, and Emotional Intelligence Coach)*

PRABHAT
PAPERBACKS

Published by
PRABHAT PAPERBACKS
An imprint of Prabhat Prakashan Pvt. Ltd.
4/19 Asaf Ali Road,
New Delhi-110 002 (INDIA)
e-mail: prabhatbooks@gmail.com

ISBN 978-93-5521-469-0
IGNITING CONSCIOUS LEADERSHIP
by Sandiip Panndit

© Sandiip Panndit

Edition
First, 2023

Price
₹ 300 (Rupees Three Hundred Only)

Printed at

Dedicated to

Maa and Baba: Thank you for being such a dedicated parents and for bringing me up and teaching me the values and principles that make me a good human being. Your belief in me filled me with strength.

With Blessings of

My Guru Babaji Neeb Karori: For showing me the path and providing me with the courage to walk on that path. It was only with your blessings that I could take a leap of faith. I am your instrument; please keep guiding me.

Foreword

Ihave been deeply and profoundly touched by the contents of this book and even more so by my relationship with Sandiip Panndit, who I got to know when I was doing Train the Trainer for Executive Coaching. Sandiip's curiosity and passion for human transformation through self-awareness struck me on the sidelines of that event. We did discuss how vital self-awareness is for all leadership coaching and how a mindful life is the genesis of a good leader. We concurred on how mastering self can lead to effective leadership.

Sandiip walks the talk and practises what he preaches. He is a seasoned professional in the field of mentoring and Consciousness Leadership. His childhood experiences are the genesis of his transformation. Sandiip has evolved and polished his Conscious Leadership framework in his three-and-a-half decades post the childhood stammering issue he overcame. Sandiip has a genuine intention and zeal to transform lives, and I have seen him closely develop powerful models that impact a person deep inside. He successfully rescues them from their lost state in life due to mid-life crisis or from leading an unfulfilled life due to lack of purpose. Sandiip's penchant for transforming individuals by showing them their hidden powers makes him unique. He says that he shows "the mirror and the map" to individuals.

As a bestselling author and the world's top Executive Coach who also coached Steve Jobs during his final days, the research organization Globalgurus.org awarded me with the prestigious world's #1 coaching authority ranking for three consecutive years – 2019, 2020, and 2021. I take these titles very humbly and seriously. I give back to this space by encouraging and nurturing coaches and mentors worldwide who are committed to their craft of mentorship. I have seen him launch his valued and successful global programs on harnessing the inner core values for finding a purpose in life to attract true success with lasting happiness. Sandiip is on a mission to bring both fulfilment and excellence to individuals and corporates.

I understood him closely, and his insights and zeal to impact individuals were evident in his engaged attention during my train-the-trainer programme. Not only that, but he was also connected with me ever since because there was a profound similarity between our work – we both believed that the inner core impacts the leadership style.

I liked Sandiip's way of approaching the subject of leadership through the conscious leadership route. That's why I endorsed his global programme – Self Mastery Code, which is now a runaway success with individuals enrolled for their holistic growth (Body, Mind, Heart, and Soul) for fulfilment.

This book on Conscious Leadership is so well-structured and well-thought-out that individuals and organizations will treasure it. The Human Resource Leaders and Learning and Development Leaders can apply this model across the organization, even as an orientation programme. Because this book carries the fundamental essence of balancing life and work to live an impactful and inspiring life with a purposeful mindset and heart-set for creativity, resilience and productivity, which are crucial for corporations along with people, planet, profit and purpose.

Some elements (self-awareness, acceptance, and forgiveness) in his Conscious Leadership framework might look simple, but they are critical and often the missing pieces of the whole puzzle. Those elements intertwine with our self-image so much that we struggle with our goals and life vision.

Sandiip has taken two steps back to re-engineer this. In this book, unlike other models, his model does not directly attempt to craft a life vision by changing your thoughts or actions. Instead, it starts from self-awareness, then self-reflection, followed by forgiveness and acceptance of what you need to take in your stride and move on to create a life vision that befits your core values, purpose, and meaning in life.

This book becomes even more touching when Sandiip shares his personal childhood experiences of emotional struggle and how he overcame it. He also shares an account of the self-image revamp he underwent after his corporate career span over the years. The vulnerabilities in this book mainly point to Sandiip's pure intention of transferring maximum value and insight to the reader.

I was highly impressed with Sandiip and how aligned we were on the impact of an individual's inner core (soul) on their outer-core skills, behaviour, impact, achievement, and ultimate success. I am in sync with Sandiip's Conscious Leadership approach, which will ignite an individual's beauty in their soul to arrive at a place of centredness, happiness, and pure joy. This model will teach you that these outcomes are not to be pursued but rather experienced, fuelled by your selflessness in creating happiness and joy in others.

With this unique approach, you can and will achieve magnificent game-changing breakthroughs in your professional and personal life! As a corporate leader, one can use this model to uplift the consciousness of their employees for an engaged, aligned, and fulfilled workforce that we genuinely need in today's times.

– John Mattone
Bestselling author of 10 books including The Executive Coach's Handbook (2022) and The Intelligent Leader (2019), the World's Top Executive Coach, and the Founder of Four Exceptional Coaching and Leadership Development Companies.

Acknowledgements

Writing a book is a journey, and if you want it to be read by thousands and hopefully millions of people, it takes considerable influence and inspiration.

For their memories, patience, and guidance, I would like to acknowledge the enormous help I received during the entire process of creating this book.

I wish to thank my brothers Anil, Sanjay, and Devesh for their constant feedback, criticism, observations, and reactions during the creation of this book.

Special acknowledgements to my friends Ritu and Vikrant for having faith in me and encouraging me to write this book. I thank them for their patience, critique, and innovative ideas, or, at times, just listening to and helping me give a perspective to my creative ideas.

Otti Vogt and Antoinette Weibel's work added one more level of validation to this book project, and I thank them for that.

The support from Geetanjali Pandit, Aditya Purandare, Ranvijay Singh, and Dr. Matt Lippincott has gone a long way in manifesting this book due to their respective and unique contributions that led to this creation.

A very special thanksgiving to the unconditional support and guidance of my mentor, John Mattone, who has just stood by me, providing me with the moral support I needed throughout.

Most importantly, I would like to convey my deep gratitude to the three people who impacted my life the most and inspired me to write: they are Dr. Wayne Dyer, Sadhguru (Founder of Isha Foundation), and Dr. Daniel Goleman.

I am deeply grateful to all those who have participated in my workshops, retreats, and sessions. Without you, there would be no life-transformation programs.

❑

Contents

RE-SCULPT

(Revamp Self-Image, Unified & Purposeful Growth)

❏

Introduction

Congratulations on prioritizing your personal growth with consciousness!

Congratulations on having a mindset to contribute to the world!

Congratulations on choosing to be a Conscious Leader!

If you have chosen this book, I know one thing: You are special and unique!

This world needs you to play an active role. It is a great synergy that the universe has put us together on the same path.

There is a seed of personal growth and contribution inside you, and now you wish to leverage the consciousness aspect to have a fulfilling life and spread that joy far and wide. You are meant to live a free life with raw and unique power deep inside. You have now decided to harness that rawness and uniqueness. That is why we are here together.

I have waited for a long time to connect with you through this book. You are holding a book in your hand that is an extract of the knowledge and experience I have distilled from the last three decades of the transformation journey. This journey has helped me to completely change my career and lifestyle, how I look at life, and how I have embraced the person I am at my core and therefore live with heightened consciousness. I have shared moments of vulnerability from my own life and how I overcame them. Besides, the book also includes my decisions, state of mind, and heart.

After 15 long years of serving in corporate roles, the turning point in my life came while I was with an IT MNC in a senior marketing role. That is when I started questioning myself. I went on a quest trying to contemplate things from a fresh perspective.

That is when I reconnected back to my core, which made me reflect and join the dots of my life. As soon as I raised my self-awareness, I was reminded of who I was during my childhood, what I loved doing, and the key drivers of my happiness and fulfilment.

I worked for two Fortune 100 companies and was in a leadership role when a situation led me to take a break from my career and undertake something I was passionate about. In hindsight, I now feel that my core values and experiences during my formative years helped me take a leap of faith.

I was intuitive as a child and loved meditation. There was a unique charm in trying out new things because, deep inside, I firmly believed in myself. I had a special connection with playgrounds, where I used to lose track of space and time. Games and sports allowed me to express myself naturally. I loved playing cricket and actively participated in almost all games and sports in school.

I was only ten years old, in Grade V, when I realized that I had developed a speech disorder — I started to stammer. My world crashed! Before this incident occurred, I loved to lead, and here I was, struggling to express myself.

I suffered in silence and extreme agony till I accepted the challenge at that early age. My parents and teachers could not gauge the quantum of my deep and perpetual suffering. I was in pain and wondered if I would ever be able to speak normally like others or if I would be left with no option but to face this challenge throughout my life. This thought sent chills down my spine.

Fast-forward three decades: I am a keynote speaker on Self-Mastery, Self-Leadership, Conscious Leadership, Mindful Living, and Living a Life of Purpose. I have touched thousands of lives across nationalities in the last ten years and transformed them from being prisoners of life to being free and fulfilled in life. My sessions and programs are an amalgamation of mindfulness, meditation, psychotherapy, and subconscious mind-power with a backing of spirituality and neuroscience.

Reading this book will either initiate a consciousness quest inside you or set you free from the unending pursuit you are experiencing, as I did when I was young. I am providing you with a trademarked and proven Soul In Harmony Conscious Leadership Framework to delve deeper, get the unique answers that apply to only you, and finally experience that heart-centred peace and harmony.

You are unique, so your solutions must also be unique, right?

My framework in this book will help you construct your own personal and distinct formula. I designed this Conscious Leadership Framework with a lot of introspection, care, and personal experiences. It has also been validated through my interactions with thousands of individuals across the spectrum whose lives I have observed inside out and transformed.

This book will set you free to achieve your dreams and save time, sweat, and wasted resources trying to crack the

code of achieving success and fulfilment together by adding a conscious element to the equation of life.

Do you think it is a simple subject?

Well, you may be right in one way.

The fact is that it is simple but not easy!

You must go through this book slowly because you need to internalize a lot. I have kept the book very simple to read and assimilate.

Do you always wonder why most people cannot balance life in terms of career, finance, health, relationships, success, happiness, peace, and so on?

They do not know the Soul In Harmony Conscious Leadership Framework I share in this book.

I have perfected something in three decades, and it has worked wonders when applied to more than forty-five thousand individuals globally.

When I decided to take a leap of faith during my childhood quest, I inadvertently sowed the seed of personal growth and started to look at life from a different perspective. Today, I am a Life Alchemist, Speaker, Mentor, and Founder of Soul in Harmony—a human transformation organization for individuals and corporates who want to unleash their excellence but are unfortunately stuck as prisoners of life.

I help individuals and corporates who believe their best is yet to come and need an alchemist to play a catalyst's role.

It is all about creating a self-awareness-based human transformation to have an inspired and fulfilling life.

I warmly welcome you on this conscious leadership journey, and I am so glad you made it here. You are an extraordinary person and are meant to do something great and leave a legacy for posterity.

I have no doubt that values such as growth, freedom, authenticity, fulfilment, and transformation are what you resonate with. You are on a quest and are a lifelong learner. You want more out of life. You wish to live to your fullest. You want to write your destiny with your hands.

Most importantly, you know deep down within that you have a hidden talent and are a kindred soul. You only need a gentle nudge. This book will do that.

And most important—you have tried a lot of self-improvement stuff already. Somehow, you have not been able to hit that 'sweet spot' of conscious leadership and therefore have not taken that leap of faith.

Am I right?

Well, this book can help you become a trailblazer to lead others using your uniqueness.

It will help you know the framework and method you can adopt and directly hack into your inner greatness to live a life of purpose and consciousness.

Disclaimer: Conscious Leadership is not a destination or a milestone. It is a journey. It is a marathon!

Remember: You cannot stop the waves, but you can learn to surf in this ocean of life. Here, I will teach you the art of surfing, so you can encounter waves in your life no matter how big they are.

The best education is self-education. And self-education with consciousness is power.

While reading this book, I would advise you not to read another self-help book simultaneously. You must maintain consistency and focus on one book at a time. Read this book slowly to internalize concepts, re-strategize your life, and finally implement with consciousness.

What to expect while reading this book and how to have the best experience?

This book is a guide to unlocking your hidden greatness. You will discover the proven **five-step framework for conscious leadership**.

- This framework will become a unique guide when applied to your situation.

- You will have insights from real-life examples and can use that to design your personalized method based on the framework.

- I will give you a proven system to unlock and embrace your unique greatness. Let me tell you that there is no ultimate formula for a truly successful life.

- You need to let the rays of your uniqueness shine through the cloud of doubts, guilt, and hesitation. In addition, you need to take the necessary action with intentionality.

- It captures unique moments, realizations, and revelations from people's lives.

- That means this conscious leadership method is validated, methodical and implementable.

- You will go on a unique, meditative and self-reflective journey. It is known that no two persons have the same meditation experience; your experience will also be unique.

Note: Try to keep a physical/digital notebook to jot down specific personal reflections as you read the book. Those natural feelings, emotions, and thoughts are the authentic

gems you need to collect as you read. If you miss it, finding those again would be a challenge.

- If you follow this book diligently, you will engage with your life meaningfully; your relationship with yourself will transform the most, exhibiting a game-changing leadership style and making you the favourite with teams and organizations.

- This will influence all the other areas of life—personal and professional relationships, social life, finance, mental and physical health, and career.

Offer to Book Readers: As a special offer to book readers, I am glad to give out some proven quickstart self-mastery tools that will get you off the mark immediately, even if you have tried a lot of stuff before.

Scan this QR Code and claim your exclusive offer available only for our readers.

For Organizations

Conscious Leadership is the need of the hour in corporations today. Self-awareness is the foundation of conscious leadership. An individual's self-awareness can empower and transform the person. An individual has the power to create a culture change in the team and family. That culture change finally affects society, organizations and the world positively. You cannot influence the world without helping individuals cultivate their self-awareness.

Self-awareness will help employees decode their life experiences and connect the dots in their personal and professional realms to leave an impact and legacy.

In the "Self-Awareness" and "Life Purpose" section, I have included what methodology leaders in organizations can implement to align their corporate objectives with individuals while maintaining a delicate balance with employees' purposeful engagement.

That becomes a panacea for individuals, teams, families and organizations.

You can expect three things clearly in this book:

1. Self-awareness – to learn who you are and what you stand for

2. Empowerment – to realize that you already have greatness within

3. Transformation – to undertake a journey to actualize that greatness

I wish you the best on your journey to becoming a conscious leader and achieving true success with fulfilment.

Amit worked in an MNC as a senior marketing professional in his mid-30s. He was a bright mid-career professional with 12 years of rich and varied experience across sales and marketing functions.

His profile required him to collaborate with his stakeholders across time zones, manage his team, and build his skills in management and leadership. He was one of the key talents any top management would love to have. On the other hand, he was going through a crisis in his personal life.

Amit was handling too many things and spreading himself too thin in his personal and professional life. He could not focus on what he wanted from his life and work. He never dared to make big decisions with so many variables and stayed within his comfort zone. The top management invited and encouraged him to take up a leadership assignment noticing his excellent work ethic and attitude, but he loathed taking risks. He feared, "What if I fail?"

Every time Amit faced a challenge at work, he would opt for a job switch. Running away from reality, clueless about his potential, he would play safe by staying within his self-made cocoon. He wrongly believed he would be sorted after switching roles, jobs, or organizations.

Too stressed, he resigned from the company in a huff, where he could have flourished as a bright leader. However, he was adamant about getting into another work environment where he could have a clean slate with a better salary. Amit missed a major opportunity.

After six months, Amit again faced the same issues at his new workplace, and he once again contemplated another job switch or starting a new business with his former colleague. One year later, he was still dissatisfied and unhappy.

What was wrong in Amit's case? Why did things keep going in a downward spiral for him despite his talent?

Amit did not have a vision of what he wanted his life to look like. As a result, his goals were only short-term ones. He often compared himself with his colleagues. Amit frequently encountered baseless self-doubts due to his mental and emotional conditionings. Due to the past, he could not let go of a few things. This block was working against him. In addition, most importantly, Amit was not mindful of his identity.

That means Amit did not have the self-awareness of who he was, what he wanted from life, why he wanted that, and how to go for it. That lack of self-awareness was the reason for all his miseries.

Can you relate to this?

Remember, it is not the life circumstances that define us, but our 'unique' responses to those circumstances certainly do.

We are all unique individuals and are meant for an extraordinary life path. It is critical to raise our self-awareness to live the authentic and powerful life we are meant to live.

We must hack into our conscious leadership and discover the purpose in life to create personal and professional excellence.

My Quest

When I graduated from college, I set the next goal: to complete my MBA from a prestigious institution and get an excellent job with a decent salary that kept growing steadily.

It was easy at first. I completed my MBA from a reputed institution, got a job in software sales, and kept getting hikes and promotions. I would often switch jobs for better opportunities.

During the first ten years of my career, I succeeded in the goal I had set up initially. Then I discovered something I had never anticipated before this point in my life. More money, new roles, new teams, or a different industry did not make me happier anymore. It might sound obvious to you, but it was challenging for me to understand back then. I believed success was about keeping a score of promotions, salary, the span of control, possessing real-estate properties, owning a nice car, and so on. This belief about happiness was not valid. *Then what was all this, I started wondering!*

I got started on a personal quest. Initially, it made me compare myself with others and look at myself through artificial lenses. That led to further beating myself up over all that I had not yet accomplished by my age. All this was like an eternal negative mysterious conundrum. It got me to do many things in between, but it became exhausting after a while.

❑

Learnings Through Life Reflections

Success versus Fulfilment

I believe it is challenging to find true success unless you prioritize fulfilment.

You can get rich, gain status, and win others' praise. However, if you are not on your life path, you might be stuck in that success, achievement, and performance conundrum yet remain unfulfilled. Does that empty success even matter?

When I think about my life and how I defined success before I realized the mistake, one thing seems constant—the moving goal posts. I considered new jobs, roles, industry, and immigration as an alibi for missing fulfilment.

These moving goal posts were like mirages that kept me in illusion. I thought the next goal post could change my life. I kept running, yet not arriving!

The fulfilment was missing because I could not hack into my consciousness to take the action that suited me as an individual.

Slow Down to Speed Up

Slow down to gain peripheral vision, and also introspect with self-awareness, look for the conditioned realities you have created, challenge to disrupt them, and create a new life vision for yourself that is in sync with your soul's purpose. I do not want you to look back at life and regret, "If only I could have done this..." A few years ago, I left a high-profile job at a company I had always admired. I have been aspiring for a career in this organization since my MBA. I was very well settled, making massive progress in my job.

But something was missing. I had lost the excitement for my work and started asking myself some serious, contemplative questions:

- Is this all there is to my career?

- Will I be happy climbing up this ladder till I retire?

- Is this the kind of career I had always envisioned?

- Am I doing justice with my talents and gifts or playing safe?

- Am I being short-sighted and afraid of the success I know I deserve?

I tried reinventing and disrupting my career for the next couple of years. I worked towards migrating, upskilling, changing schedules and shifting industries, business units, and roles.

The harder I tried, the more desperate I became. I was getting disconnected from the career I once felt was my dream path. At a point, I decided to release the career-related beliefs I had created on my own and was holding on to with a tight fist.

After months of navigating through my quest and letting things show up on their own, I found a new outlet—an opportunity to work on something entirely different yet innate to me. This

29

was way beyond my comfort zone. A new challenge, you can say!

Initially, it was intimidating. Back then, I had no personal mentor who could have given me unbiased validation of what was suitable for me. But thankfully, I did much soul-searching and followed my quest to connect with who I was deep within. Finally, I found my sweet spot and took a leap of faith because many serendipities pointed me clearly to where I should be moving.

Today's times are different as people are open to exploring, and you find inspired mentors who can help you navigate these personal and professional bottlenecks. In India, back in 2010, the term Life Coach was new, so I did not find a mentor who had walked the path and made it successful as a coach or mentor after quitting his corporate career.

But I had gone through a churn, and deep inside, I knew what resonated with me. I wanted to give back to those mid-career professionals who are on a quest to rekindle their passion in their work and life. I knew their pressure points, the aspects they might be missing out on, the tunnel vision they might have been conditioned to, and the immense fear of venturing out of their comfort zone.

I knew how they were being prisoners of life!

They deserved freedom, and I knew one thing for sure—I could transform them to live an impactful and fulfilling life.

I connected with more profound passion, core values, life experiences, and key strengths to discover the meaning of my unique fulfilment. **(Now, refer to the Introduction of this book in case you have skipped it).**

Very Important Disclaimer:

For the kind of person I was, my core values of freedom, authenticity, and growth did not match my corporate career.

Therefore, I was unfulfilled in continuing my old career trajectory. **I am not recommending you quit your corporate career!**

All I invite you to do is slow down to speed up in the long run. Look within and find your true essence! I have explained this clearly in Conscious Leadership Stage 5 – Unified & Purposeful Growth.

In 2010, I became a Life Coach and guided working professionals to have a self-awareness-based personal transformation to carve an inspiring and fulfilling life.

These qualities of mine as a coach and mentor have always surfaced intermittently in my life, even during my school and college days.

I quit my corporate career after working for 15 years and serving in leadership roles across different corporations, industries, functions, and roles. I learned a lot throughout my career, and the learnings help me to this day in my entrepreneurial venture. I felt saturated in that environment and was certainly not thriving.

After five years of successful practice, I finally registered my venture, Soul in Harmony, which helped individuals and corporates. In India, it was a lesser-known concept from 2010–15. Everything was new for me. The work scenario changed, the friend circle became limited and different, my social life transformed, and my schedules changed. My lifestyle evolved into something I always wished for but could not define initially.

And a surprising thing happened—I started loving myself when I observed my life bringing meaning to others' lives.

I rekindled my passion at work!

Somehow, my income levels had dropped slightly for some time, but my fulfilment quotient had multiplied! Now, I am glad I slowed down to listen to myself because I am fulfilled in every way!

Reminder Disclaimer

This is my story; as you know, every individual has a unique journey. I am only urging you to connect with your inner selves fearlessly to know who you are and the qualities you are born with.

For me, the dots connected back to work outside a corporate career. This might not be the case for all of you. Some of you might be poised to be the best salesperson in the world, some might become like Sundar Pichai (the top CEO of the world), or others might become the best software programmer in the world or a renowned musician, and so on.

Later in this book, I will give you a complete Soul In Harmony Conscious Leadership Framework to find your fulfilling work and create a life that is inspiring and fulfilling.

Pull These Five Levers for Fulfilment

In general, there are five planes of fulfilment:

- Financial (external)

- Create an impact (external)

- Connect to core values (internal)

- Link to the purpose (internal)

- Utilize talents (internal)

You need to deep-dive, observe and contemplate the one that matches your soul.

We all have our motives for doing what we do for work. Some motives are generated artificially by observing others, like money, titles, where we work, connections, and benefits.

But I have realized now that in most cases, people who pursued only the external factors ended up unfulfilled, leaving a mysterious emotional void.

The motives or factors that come from within are the keys to unlocking joyfulness and fulfilment in our lives.

Viktor Frankl, the holocaust survivor and a renowned Austrian neurologist, psychiatrist, philosopher, and writer, wrote in his book *Man's Search for Meaning,* **"Those who have a 'why' to live can bear with almost any 'how.'"**

I have realized this is so true!

During mentoring and coaching, I have encountered unhappy and struggling entrepreneurs after they were funded, MNC C-suites quitting jobs to work in non-profits, and individuals in secure and robust perks-driven government jobs contemplating voluntary retirement. This entire emotional void erupted later in life because the race they ran for two or three decades was never theirs. So, they were not happy even after winning the race and looked for something else. So, to each his own; there is no single answer to fulfilment.

People became happier as they inched closer to the roles that used their talents, making them contribute to this planet, something they were passionate about. In most cases, they initially made less money and did less glamorous work. But the ease and quality of life rose steeply. This led to other related positive synchronicities.

As strange as it may sound to you, the fact is that it is not the money or status that makes us fulfilled; instead, the things that allow us to be ourselves lead to fulfilment. I will address this very point from multiple perspectives in this book.

Are You Searching For Your Answers?

It is nothing new for people to be on a quest.

- What is my purpose and meaning in life?

- How can I be both successful and happy?

- What is the most suitable career for me?

- Why is my life filled with struggle and strife?

- Why does money keeps eluding me?

These questions have challenged and intrigued people for centuries. Thankfully, many people have deep-dived into this quest and have shared their experiences in some form or other. In addition, we can learn so much from exploring other people's struggles, commentaries, and experiences on similar topics.

I am still very much on my journey of personal development. However, I have unfolded a few of the answers and a ton of newer questions during the process by digging deep into this area of a purposeful and fulfilling life. Mere observation, discussion, and consultation with people who have faced these questions gave me new perspectives to look at life. Thanks to those people and the situations that helped me open up to the answers instead of just living in my head.

These are tough questions to wrestle with. However, it is worth it. I share the same wisdom to help you navigate your unique life.

If you are like most others, you are used to planning for achievement, or what I call 'head-based successes.' If you are unlike them, you need to prepare to get inspired and find your life's purpose for 'heart-based successes' called fulfilment. This requires designing your life with a purpose in mind.

Exercise 1

Some questions you must ask yourself for your fulfilment space: -

1. What are your core values?

2. Is the work you do/or that you want to do, aligned with your values?

3. How can you get your work to be more aligned with your values?

4. What is important to you as an individual?

5. What does fulfilment mean to you?

6. Visualize yourself as a well-rounded, balanced, versatile individual. How does 'that life' appear to you?

7. What areas of your life do you need to work on now to get you to be more balanced?

8. What does the quality of life mean to you?

9. How can you have more quality of life?

10. What actions can you take today to get closer to a more 'self-fulfilled you'?

11. Remember a time when you were successful at something? How did you feel? How do you feel now when you remember that occasion?

12. Remember a time when you felt fulfilled. How did you feel? How do you feel now remembering that occasion?

13. Do self-fulfilment and success feel the same to you? Is there a difference between the two?

14. Tell me what you want to be ten years later. Self-fulfilled or successful? Neither/both?

15. When do you want to be successful?

16. When do you want to be self-fulfilled?

Conscious Leadership, Purpose, and Fulfilment

Conscious leadership is a revolutionary and impactful technique where leaders practise being aware of themselves and the environment — how they think, respond, and view the world. It is a practise where leaders mindfully navigate themselves and their team through a growth path in an inclusive and allied approach instead of an egocentric and aggressive approach.

Conscious leadership is a continuous practice of understanding who you are, identifying your aligned future experiences, and intentionally navigating yourself towards them no matter what. It involves determining what, why, and how you do it.

Your purpose in life works as a compass for your ultimate fulfilment. Nothing else will give you a feeling of alignment with your inner core as a 'purpose in life' does.

Conscious leadership includes an internally regulated choice (what), value alignment (why), and execution of the chosen activity (how).

Fig. 2.1 : **What is Conscious Leadership?** Conscious Leadership includes value alignment (why you do certain things), an internally regulated choice (what you choose to do), and execution of the chosen activity (how you do them).

Conscious leadership leads to sustainable growth and harmony. Furthermore, as explained earlier, fulfilment is rooted in self-awareness combined with self-reflection, acceptance, self-image enhancement and purposeful growth.

Conscious leadership is based on the realization that there are parts of us that will always try to hold us back. Our biggest naysayers aren't "out there"; they are within us.

Someone committed to the path of conscious leadership is willing to find ways to transcend their fears and forge a breakthrough for themselves and others as a cohesive unit.

Conscious leadership implies that deep inside, one possesses the self-awareness necessary to identify the source of one's resistance and the creativity to find a mindful path and purposefully navigate through it.

The conscious leadership journey starts from 'where you are' and strives to keep going purposefully towards 'where you plan to reach' in a value-based manner.

It is a heart-centred, purpose-driven, values-focused leadership style that starts with an inward-facing approach.

Five Stages of Conscious Leadership

1. **Self-awareness**: Develop **self-awareness** to find your authentic self. Who are you? What are your thoughts? What are your feelings or emotions? What is your environment?

2. **Self-reflection**: Pause for **self-reflection** and get to know yourself. This includes reflecting on your weaknesses, strengths, and life experiences.

3. **Acceptance and Forgiveness**: Cultivate **acceptance** towards people who have hurt you and for situations that hold you back in life to reconcile differences and reduce dissonance successfully. Reflect on what you have gone through and what you are willing to let go of.

4. **Revamp self-image**: Revamp the **self-image** to transcend from being a self-critic to **tapping into your hidden uniqueness.** How do you perceive yourself? Have you spotted your negative conditioning?

5. **Unified & Purposeful Growth**: Get onto your purpose in life and be on an unending path of **growth** to own your hidden greatness. Alongside, ally with the team and others with a **purposeful approach for unified growth.** How can you create a life vision that is true to yourself? What is your purpose in life? How can you align your purpose and values with your team and the organization?

I will explain each of these five stages in detail. So, keep going—read, reflect, note down, plan, implement and experience!

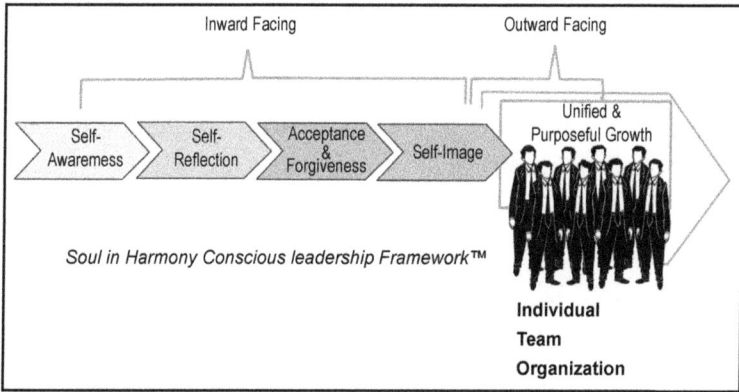

Fig. 2.2 : **5 Stages of Soul In Harmony Conscious Leadership™**
*This Conscious Leadership framework combines 5 steps The first 4 steps
are inward-facing, and only the last step is outward-facing. This shows how
essential it is for us as individuals to go within ourselves to be
truly successful to lead effectively.*

Take Your Pathway to Fulfilment

Fulfilment comes when you hone your conscious leadership. Conscious leadership is a journey to work and optimize your life for holistic growth that uniquely belongs to you. Holistic life refers to having true success, lasting happiness, and inner peace.

Conscious leadership works through self-awareness and helps to remove the false layers that are not serving you. When those layers are removed, you can see, accept and be the person you are and do what you are truly capable of doing.

Our brain is an ultra-sophisticated device like a supercomputer. When we talk about goal visualization, the feeling generated while visualizing the goal achievement is the one thing that matters most. It needs to be worthy and resonate with your core, the person you are. Therefore, it requires tremendous self-awareness and self-reflection.

Note: I will later explain life vision. It is not the same as a goal.

Know the Difference: End Goal vs. Means Goal

You need to understand the concept of end goal and means goal. This will let you align yourself and focus on the right objectives.

An end goal is an outcome you hope to accomplish with your actions. Those action steps are also known as means goals. So, ask yourself three to five times, "Why?" and you will arrive at an 'end goal'.

I recommend you have end goals and not the means goals.

Earlier I used to create means goals such as getting a well-paying role in a multinational corporation.

If you have a similar goal, ask yourself why you need that kind of role.

The answer is to have a stable career, sound learning, and a chance to travel more to experience life.

Ask yourself further why you need a stable career, sound learning, and a chance to travel more.

The answer is to grow faster and have an acceptable/ respectable lifestyle.

Therefore, the end goal is 'to grow faster and have a decent lifestyle'.

The end goal can be supported by the means goal, which is a stable career in an MNC.

If you start focusing on the means goals, you know everything, including how that end goal can be achieved. But often, that might not happen because you have tunnel vision. If we set a plan based on the end goal, our brains are free to find multiple ways to achieve those goals rather than being constrained by only a few specified means.

Know the Power of Intention

"Our intention creates our reality."

– Dr. Wayne Dyer

An intention in alignment with thought and action creates the desired outcome. And if you are stuck, you must review the thinking and actions that resulted in the present undesired circumstances or situation you are stuck in.

In the universe, there is an immeasurable, indescribable force called intent, and absolutely everything in the cosmos is attached to intent by a connecting chord. Individuals can do amazing things when animated by intention and purpose. Accessing this force field of energy requires connecting with your natural self. That is where conscious leadership comes into action.

• What if you could get clarity on the outcome you seek – your end goal?

• How would it feel to know that every little action you take gets you to a place you intend to go?

• You do not want just to accomplish daily to-dos for its sake. You seek results like losing weight, becoming healthy, starting a business, monetizing your passion, or mending a critical relationship.

• You do not just want a job in an MNC for its sake. You desire stability, lifestyle, and extraordinary growth to experience life at all levels.

• You do not just want to build a money business. Instead, your clear intention is to solve a burning problem using your talents and resources to create a meaningful life that will give you fulfilment and keep you financially secure.

But most of the time, you do not intentionally define those underlying outcomes and their cause. That makes your daily action steps misleading and, more importantly, leads to autopilot and uninspired delusional life.

Remember that your ability to activate the power of intention in your life depends on being commensurate with your creative source. If you fail to match up, the power of intention eludes you.

Our subconscious mind and nature work in tandem, and our subconscious mind is fully dedicated when we are entirely in harmony with the end goal we have set for ourselves.

Whenever you look back in retrospect on your significant accomplishments, you can feel there was no way you could have planned it the way it happened. Your present life is the interplay between these two aspects – your intention and your subconscious mind.

Steve Jobs said, "You can connect the dots by only looking backwards."

Every present moment has a future embedded into it because you create your future only in the present. Therefore, you need to guard your subconscious mind against unwanted thoughts. You will become your party spoiler if you do not take care of it.

Most of us go about our daily life mechanically and get carried by the winds of circumstance. If something happens, we fret and fume out of displeasure or yell and cheer from joy, but we generally just let whatever happens to guide our direction in life. And if we ever try to achieve something, we rarely put all our mental energy into it.

Rishita, one of my clients and a senior corporate professional from a premier B-School, was getting into the wrong relationships and suffering each time. This was causing immense pressure on her professional career and social life. It was not till we worked together on her self-image to allow her to reset her mental and emotional programming that she met a man of her choice and ultimately got married.

The critical issue is that you tend to place your fate in the hands of uncontrollable forces. And, surely, there will be many things you will be unable to control, and therefore you should learn to adapt to them as they arise. However, you can take control of many aspects of your life thanks to the power of intention and your power of choice.

When focusing our mental energy on something, we can give more of our brainpower to it. It is not magic or hocus-pocus; our brain's Reticular Activation System (RAS) is primed to perform at maximum efficiency. It is as simple as that!

Must-Know 10 Principles for Conscious Leadership

Here are ten principles to strive and guide you on this conscious leadership journey.

1. **Craft a compelling personal vision:** You need a compass to reach your destination. Of course, you will have a solid intention to achieve a defined goal. That destination forms your life vision, which will act as a compass as you undertake this journey.

2. **Accept that you would face resistance to growth; everyone does:** You can save yourself a lot of guilt and shame and avoid unnecessary obstacles if you accept your resistances and impediments upfront as and when they arise. These enduring moments are when you rewire your brain and change the already existing negative self-talk. And at the same time, you are honing your resilience by enduring the pain caused by a challenge.

3. **Commit to long-term practice:** Conscious leadership is not a sprint but a marathon. If you commit to a long-term approach in the areas you want to improve, you will be less likely to give up when you hit plateaus. Micro progress over a long period has the power to create massive shifts and breakthroughs. I am sure you know that there is incredible power in compounding. Albert Einstein once said, "Compounding is the world's eighth wonder."

4. **Expect to backslide:** Backsliding is inevitable on the path to growth and conscious leadership. Life happens, and we do fall into an abyss inadvertently. If you know this, you will be less discouraged when entering such a phase because you know that this is also a part of

the deal. Real success, when plotted on a graph, looks shabby. You will sometimes trip and fall, backslide, or feel uninspired, but if you know this is a normal phenomenon, you will start crawling, walking, running, or flying ahead very soon.

5. **Live by the principle of moderation:** When you push or strain yourself, you induce involuntary tension in your Sympathetic Nervous System (SNS). We tend to get into a fight, flight or freeze mode during intense stress. The SNS prevents us from staying open, relaxed, and engaged while avoiding extremes. As you know, excess of anything is bad. For example, being quality-oriented is good. Still, suppose you keep striving for perfection endlessly and missing out on life; then this same quality consciousness results in your ill health, and you and your employer will suffer. On the other hand, if you can balance your zeal for perfection within limits, you can be a consistent performer, enjoy the process of creation, enjoy life, and make consistent strides in your career growth.

6. **Lighten up:** This is continued from the above point of 'the principle of moderation.' In addition to not living in extremes, we must enjoy the process. And what is the best way to do that? By lightening up, sprucing up your life with something that makes you forget the workload or the current challenges at the workplace or in relationships.

Watch the choicest movie with your loved ones, cook your favourite dish for a change, or play a sport that lets you de-stress. If you continue upping the ante for your work, you will invariably derail your efforts if you take yourself seriously. Have fun on this journey. Pause and check your feelings from time to time. Ask

49

for feedback from your loved ones; ask them if you are getting too mechanical or boring, whose company is no more attractive. This helps you to stay grounded.

7. **Set mini-goals:** For conscious leadership, you do not need to aim at only massive outcomes daily. Instead, learn to continue taking those baby steps on the path to your life vision and keep knocking off the small hurdles each day. Remember that while a compelling life vision keeps you focused and inspired, mini-goals can help you keep going and keep you aware of your progress.

8. **Cultivate physical energy:** No matter which road you take to conscious leadership, you need a healthy reserve of physical strength to help manage stress, overcome resistance, and follow through. The golden rule is to keep your body movement a daily priority. Body movement is a critical first step in managing your emotions. Focus on nutrition, supplements, and body movement to keep an excellent physical energy reserve.

9. **Assess yourself honestly:** Self-assessment is essential for anyone on the path. We often invest tremendous energy in lying to others and ourselves. Instead, I invite you to be brutally honest with yourself while you do your self-assessment periodically.

10. **Establish empowering practices:** For a leader, they need to have a like-minded circle. This will help the leader to keep moving ahead despite hurdles and obstacles. That will aid you in institutionalizing empowering rituals that suit you best. Practices allow us to sustain this challenging journey by building long-term resilience and commitment to our life vision. High achievers in every field have routines for getting into the ideal mindset to perform at their best.

Pump Up Your Life Energetically

Quantum Tool #1

• **Turn up your frequency**

The higher my frequency, the easier my dreams will flow to me. The energy I put out will be the energy I get back.

Four easy ways to turn up the energy vibration are as follows:

1. Exercise (Body)

2. Mindfulness (Mind)

3. Acceptance, Love, Compassion and Playfulness (Heart)

4. Meditation, Purpose and meaning in life (Soul)

Quantum Tool #2

• **Set a powerful intention to align with love or a feeling whose frequency is above love. (Example: joy, peace, enlightenment).**

We, as human beings, have an ebb and flow of life. At times, we feel low, and that is fine. Acknowledge, look at it objectively, and go through it with love, joy, and peace. When we do not resist and just go through life with these feelings, we let them pass gently instead of creating a conflict and building up suffering in the temporary challenge in life. Just focus on embracing and learning from the phase by aligning with feelings of love, joy, and peace.

Dr. David R. Hawkins created a map on the scales of human consciousness: the ego's different levels of manifestation. He then provides a guide to transcending the ego's limitation and where one may be stuck along the process of awakening to higher states of consciousness.

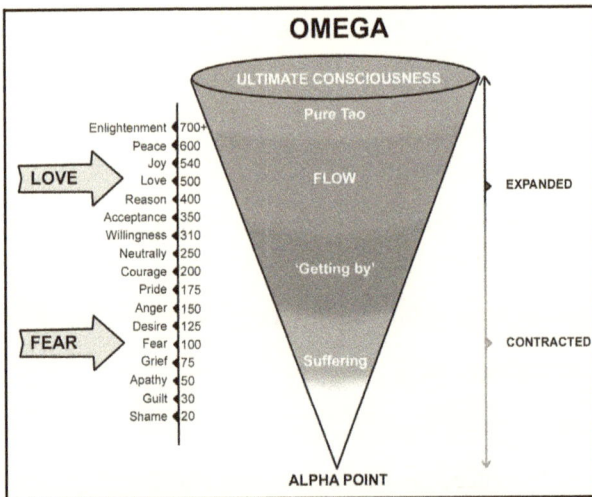

Fig. 2.3 : *The Hawkins Scale of Consciousness*
Dr. David R Hawkins created a map on the scales of human consciousness,
which is the ego's different levels of manifestation.

Quantum Tool #3

• **Shift your energy to what brings you joy**

Close your eyes, take two deep breaths, and ask yourself: What would I do if I could be, have, do, and create anything? What is my deepest desire? How would I be feeling, and to whom would I be impacting?

You are connected to your heart's desire and soul, not just the logical mind. Stay focused on the highest version of who you are and what you are meant for.

Quantum Tool #4

• **Surround yourself with people who elevate your energy and feel positively towards you.**

Surround yourself with people who lift you, lend you knowledge, and help you learn from your mistakes. Raise the standard of your inner circle. We have discussed the importance of a like-minded tribe or kindred spirits in the earlier section.

A world-renowned motivational speaker and coach said, "You are the average of five people you spend the most time with."

Surrounding yourself with relevant people can affect every aspect of your life, from career and business to social life and romantic relationships. When you surround yourself with positivity, you are more likely to adopt empowering beliefs and see life as happening 'for you' instead of 'to you'. Just as you benefit when you surround yourself with people who make you happy, you suffer when you have negative and closed-minded folks around you.

Quantum Tool #5

- **Stand firm for the things that matter to you – Quitting is not on your choice list.**

In case of weight loss, financial growth, career growth, relationships, and finances, operate from the point that everything is in control and will work out in your favour. I leave you with this thought: Where would you like to step-up in your life? Pick a category.

For example, career, business, relationships, family, health, prosperity, or lifestyle.

There is no circumstance, no person, and no place with the full power to take you out of your natural positive energy source. You are the only person who can control your frequency, and this book is here to guide and support you to do that, despite all odds.

When you feel you have reached the saturation point of suffering, push your threshold slightly higher. You would be surprised to see the man or woman you have become. The

Hawkins' Scale helps us understand how emotional frequency matters to us on our path to enlightenment.

Remember that enlightenment is not a binary 'Yes' or 'No.'

While many think that "enlightenment" is a single state of mind that you either "have" or not, it is much more helpful to think of enlightenment in terms of a process or a scale of consciousness.

Deal with Overthinking – Three Circles Model Approach

This approach helps in dealing with your overthinking and staying focused in life. If you do not curb your overthinking tendencies, you unnecessarily spend time and energy focusing on things that do not align with your life.

This model will make you live life with intentionality. As a result, you concentrate on the right things better. You can be more productive, control your emotions and reactions and let go of anything that does not add up to your intention and the person you are at your core. This requires a well-cultivated self-awareness. That is the reason we emphasize self-awareness when we talk about conscious leadership.

Let me explain to you the Three Circles Model.

1. **Circle of Concern:** This is the outermost concentric circle. This contains situations you have no direct control over but are still concerned about. For example, celebrity gossip, war, politics, news, government activities and the global economy. There is no need to spend time on these matters because you cannot change them directly.

2. **Circle of Influence:** These areas of life we can directly influence. This is where you tap into your intentionality by using your self-awareness to determine what you want to create in your life (after knowing who you are and where you want to take your life). For example, a promotion at work, holistic health, business success, children's well-being, upskilling for the future, attitude towards success, family bonding, and so on. This is where you plan and strategize life.

3. **Circle of Control:** This is the innermost circle. In this circle, there are things we can control directly based on what we have prioritized in the Circle of Influence.

For example, where you live, whom you meet, what you eat, what you buy, what you read, where you invest, how much you sleep, what you think, and so on.

This is where your execution lies because your implementation is derived from your Circle of Influence. This is a vital circle, and the daily action and moment-to-moment awareness are leveraged from this circle.

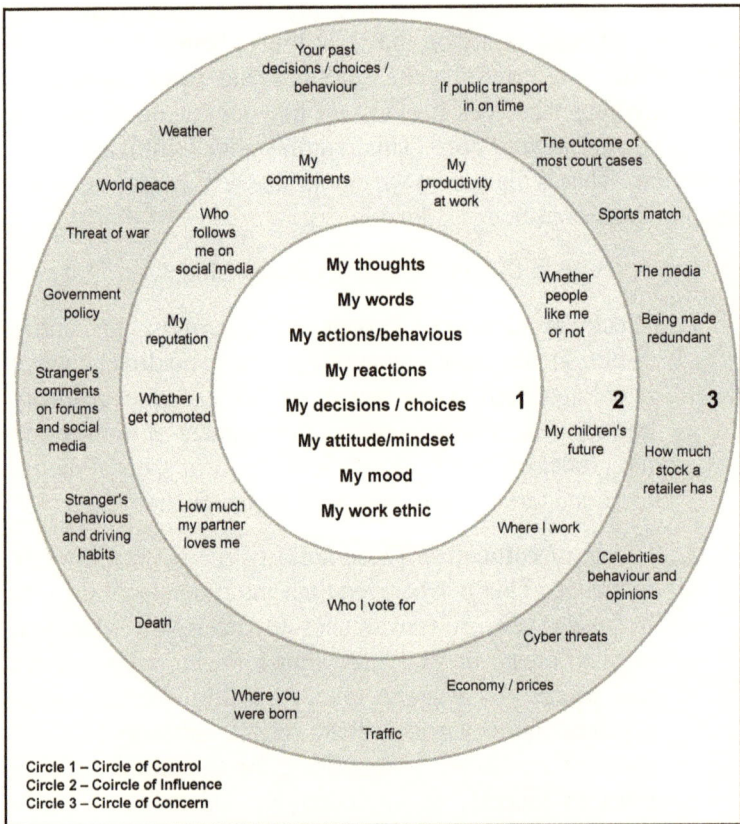

Circle 1 – Circle of Control
Circle 2 – Coircle of Influence
Circle 3 – Circle of Concern

*Fig. 2.4 : **3 Circles Model to Curb Overthinking***
The 3 Circles Model helps to focus on the things that matter with intentionality in life. This helps in cultivating a moment-to-moment awareness and avoiding unnecessary thinking.

Summary

Proactive people focus their efforts on their Circle of Influence and Control. They work on the things they can do something about: health, children, problems at work, career aspirations, business expansion, and so on.

- Reactive people focus their efforts on the circle of concern they have almost no control over. It includes the national debt, terrorism, weather, etc.

- Gaining an awareness of the areas in which we expend our energies is a giant step in becoming proactive.

- The more you have in your Circle of Concern, the more ineffective you will be.

- The more you have in your Circle of Influence and Control, the more effective you will be in creating the life you want, and people will trust and follow you.

You only become a leader for others when you become effective and impactful in your own life.

Distinguish between the "Have's and the Be's"

One more way of looking at the Three Circles Model is this:

We could determine which circle our thoughts belong to and mindfully shift our thoughts to the Circle of Influence and Circle of Control.

Distinguish between the 'Have's and the Be's.'

The Circle of Concern is filled with 'Have' — these are the things you have no control over.

For example,

- If only I could have my house paid off, I would have done...

57

- If only I had a more patient husband, I would have become...

- If only I could have more time, I would have completed...

- If only I could have more money, I would have started...

The Circle of Influence is filled with the Be's – these are your priority areas.

- I can be more patient

- I can be wise

- I can be loving

- I can be more resourceful

- I can be more diligent

- I can be more creative

- I can be more cooperative

Over-analysing the past and over-worrying about the future leads us to suffer in the NOW. It is like tying a heavy, burdensome iron weight to your feet, weighing you down.

A Philosophical thought: How to reduce your suffering?

Remember the equation, P*R=S

P = **Pain**

R = **Resistance**

S = **Suffering**

We are born on this planet because we need to evolve through pain. So, **pain** is the prop provided to all of us for our growth. And **pain** is a constant because we all have our unique threshold of **pain**. The point depends on the person we are and our life experiences.

So, the only variable in this equation is **resistance**. If we wish to decrease our **suffering**, we will need to lower our **resistance** to events and situations happening in our lives. Therefore, in other words, we need to increase our **acceptance** to decrease our **suffering**.

❑

RELOOK
(Self-Awareness, Self-Reflection and Acceptance)

RELOOK
(Self-Awareness, Self-Reflection and Acceptance)

Conscious Leadership Stage One — Self-Awareness

"No one can see their reflection in running water. It is only in still water that we can see."

– Taoist Proverb

"To become different from what we are, we must be aware of what we are."

– Bruce Lee

If you want to lose weight but are unaware of how many calories you consume through meals or burn off through everyday activities, it is hard to know exactly which aspect to change to see the desired results. You need to be aware of so many levers for weight reduction. Eating right is just one of them.

This is one key reason why weight loss is so challenging. It is easy to eat mindlessly without awareness of the nutritional value of the food, and it is easy to have a sedentary lifestyle without tracking activity. Without self-awareness, you will not know which lever to pull and how much.

The same logic works for getting promoted and a salary hike. You need to be intentional and mindful of which levers to control, isn't it?

This now brings us to our key and most foundational topic – self-awareness!

What Is Self-Awareness?

- Who are we?

- What are our emotions?

- How do others see us?

- How do we fit into this world?

With the self-awareness trait, we can answer the above questions.

If you are self-aware, you can objectively self-assess, regulate your emotions, align your actions with your values and understand how others perceive you. In other words, as a self-aware person, you can objectively understand and interpret your actions, feelings, and thoughts.

Self-awareness is critical to increasing job satisfaction levels, becoming an impactful leader, improving relationships, managing your emotions, and so on. It also significantly contributes to happiness and joyfulness in the personal, social, and professional realms.

Yet, as one research estimates, only 10–15 per cent of people are truly self-aware. Fortunately, self-awareness can be practised and cultivated as it is not a trait you are born with.

Self-awareness is now the latest buzzword in the corporate health and well-being arena, and it is so for good reasons.

Research in the last three-four decades has proved that self-awareness improves us as human beings in all three realms, namely, personal, social, and professional.

You are unique, and you deserve to know every aspect of your uniqueness to lead the life you are meant to live.

Some of us might discard these self-inquiry questions as philosophical thoughts. Still, that means you will never feel defeated if you have harnessed self-awareness and are aware of who you are, what you are meant for, and what your environment is. Despite 'losing everything,' if such a moment comes, you will still have the inner strength and resilience to recreate a beautiful life that others can dream about. That is because you know things so well, why something unfortunate happened and what suits you in the new scheme. I say this with real-life experience!

After completing my MBA from a premier Business School, I had fifteen years of corporate career experience. When I was in a job in an organization that was ranked in the Top 5 of Fortune 500 companies, which also happened to be my dream career during my MBA days, I decided to move on to another direction in my life. This direction would provide me with fulfilment.

'How was this possible?' In almost all my programs or workshops on self-mastery and conscious leadership, people often ask me this.

Well, the simple and straight answer to this oft-asked question is – that I raised my self-awareness to a higher level. The detailed nuances of this statement are what this whole book is about. My experiences mixed with my clients, plus extensive reading and observation on self-awareness, has led me to infer that even if you do everything 'right' and miss cultivating your self-awareness, those 'rights' don't matter anyway.

When Nothing Helped, Mindfulness Did

Many changes occurred when I attempted to cultivate self-awareness to find my path.

Some of the concurrent positive ramifications were as follows:

- I got to know my core values – i.e. what drives me as a person.

- Looking back, I connected my life experiences with what life was trying to draw me towards.

- I finally stopped suppressing my soul's voice, paid attention to it, and eventually took action.

- I could remove my bias and prejudice to measure my success based on societal norms.

- I developed a broader vision and a more profound outlook on life.

- I stopped having tunnel vision by deleting the damaging programs I had unknowingly installed in childhood.

- I started following a guiding light (my soul's voice) fearlessly that resided within me.

- And finally, the magic happened – I could clearly see my life path and mission.

Outer success without spiritual triumph is like a moon without the stars.

Ayn Rand, a writer and philosopher, encouraged us to live with "clear sight and a clean soul".

Our culture has trained us to seek worldly success—often at the cost of inner peace. When we become self-aware, we start giving importance to inner peace and spiritual triumph. Mindfulness practice is what helps cultivate self-awareness.

I saw the magic unfold only after I started practising mindfulness. I would like to mention that I started meditating by myself in childhood. I got many breakthroughs from it during my formative years.

However, mindfulness broadened my horizon of life and transformed my life experiences. I moved from 'doing things to look good to others' to 'doing the right things to be relaxed and joyful.'

Let me tell you, this was no mean feat, and I know its importance now. It has made my life free-flowing, so I am often connected with myself. Whenever I am not, I sense that, too.

That self-awareness trait is what mindfulness practice has given me. Therefore, I know the power of mindfulness practice.

Rear-view mirror concept: If we drive looking at the rear-view mirror, we are most likely to crash into the lamp post.

Can You Risk Your Body and Mind to This Extent?

Today, we live in a volatile, uncertain, complex, and ambiguous (VUCA) world where the lines between personal, social, and professional life blur increasingly. There is immense overlap between these three aspects of our life. The only thing that keeps us relevant in the many roles we perform as individuals is the presence of self-awareness in all facets of life.

You cannot stop the waves, but you can learn to surf. So, self-awareness will help you learn to surf the waves while keeping yourself afloat. In the waves of change, you will find your direction. Consequently, self-awareness will allow you to harness self-awareness and navigate to where you are meant to be.

An average human body has ~ 40 trillion cells. When stressed out for just one second, there are $40*(10^18)$ adverse chemical reactions throughout the human body. Imagine the damage it can cause to a person stressed-out for an hour, a day, a week, a month, a year, or a decade. Will you ever allow this destruction consciously to your body and mind?

Remember that our mind and body are intricately interconnected!

Individuals Benefit from Self-Awareness

When an individual (or an employee) embraces self-awareness, it helps them with a higher emotional intelligence leading to self-care, self-compassion, care for others, compassion, and integrity. People stay true to themselves and others. Self-awareness endorses individuals attempting to live their values fully in the work they perform.

Organizational citizenship is a kind of role that is not part of one's formal job description but plays a significant and key role in organizational productivity and effectiveness. Self-awareness creates the foundation of organizational citizenship and works equally well for organizations, as shared in the earlier section. An employee gains intrinsic satisfaction as it raises 'belonging and self-esteem' needs while gratifying his sense of purpose and meaning in his professional life and life as a whole. From a social point of view, self-awareness enables employees to handle multiple job demands, unexpected job roles, and high workloads through interdependence.

Self-awareness creates corporate citizenship and then acts as an essential indicator suggesting an employee's satisfaction, commitment, and involvement in an organization's success. It is more so when one aligns their spirituality and self-awareness with the organization's goal, which means the individual is not just concerned about their task performance but also exerts additional efforts to ensure that their team, department, and the organization as a whole achieves its target.

Emotional Intelligence (EI) has gained recognition in the last two decades in organizational settings. Thanks to Dr. Daniel Goleman for coining Emotional Quotient (EQ) in 1995. He was the first to research and share his findings with the world. Through that research, Dr. Goleman suggested that the Emotional

Quotient is more important than Intelligence Quotient (IQ), even in organizations.

Emotions as a "feeling aspect" provide invaluable information about self, associated people, and the interpersonal transactions inside the organizational atmosphere. By tapping into the rich information on emotions, especially the degree of Emotional Intelligence (EI), one can alter the thinking and behaviour to negotiate organizational challenges productively and adaptively. However, organizations often ignore this "feeling" aspect of organizational functioning, thus making emotional connectedness a less effective strategy.

An individual's takeaways:

1. You will become more creative because you are open to more possibilities.

2. You can live a more fulfilling life because you are not tethered to the societal view of success.

3. You become more fearless because you are in touch with your hidden powers.

4. You will become objective and relevant because you are not living in the past or future.

5. You will express yourself more meaningfully and see your tribe grow.

6. You feel more relevant in your life's personal, social, and professional aspects.

7. You will become a creator of your life, working on yourself each moment by cultivating self-awareness.

John C. Maxwell, the renowned author, coach, and speaker on leadership, said, "A leader is the one who knows the way, goes the way, and shows the way."

Is it not true that to become a leader in the world, we need to learn and master ourselves? Then the obvious question arises – What trait do we need to understand ourselves? That trait is self-awareness!

Move from Knowing to Doing to Being

The fact is—if you do not cultivate self-awareness and somehow, let us say, you get your finances right, you might end up losing all that and much more in the end.

Let me share a real-life incident that flashed across the media a few years ago. The winner of the TV series Kaun Banega Crorepati (Fifth Season), Sushil Kumar, won rupees five crores in 2011. However, by 2015 he revealed in his interview:

* 2015–16 was the most challenging time of my life. I didn't know what to do.

* Many people cheated me.

* I got addicted to alcohol and smoking.

* News about my bankruptcy spread like wildfire.

Why do you think a person who won the rupees five crore prize unexpectedly lost his entire money and peace of mind within four years? The reason is worth noting.

Mr. Sushil's energy and self-awareness were not a suitable match for the vast, unexpected amount of money. Quantum Theory by the famous German physicist Max Planck illustrates that everything is energy. We will discuss this elaborately later in this book. As of now, let us understand it this way.

We need to match our frequency (and sustain that frequency long enough) to the things we seek in life. We must move from 'knowing' to 'doing' to 'being'. Once there is a match, it creates resonance, and nature bestows that on us. And when we lose that vibration, the things we receive from mother nature move out of our life. This is what exactly happened with Mr. Kumar.

And the final question is – why did Mr. Kumar's energy not match his new prosperous identity?

Because self-awareness was lacking in his new life situation after receiving the prize money. Later, when Mr. Kumar regained his self-awareness and grounded himself in the new situation, he became truly fulfilled. His self-awareness ensured that he moved from knowing to doing to being himself. He reunited with his family and established himself in a career that suited him the most.

Be Curious

When you are curious, you are naturally highly involved in the process. And when you are intrinsically involved in the process, you tap into a beautiful and soothing self-awareness space. That is how you can naturally drift into a state of being where you are in the present moment—neither regretful of the past nor curious about the future.

Let us say you want to work on your anger issues.

Become curious and ask a few questions yourself:

- Which issues have mostly made me angry and resentful in the past?

- What triggered that anger at the moment?

- How did I feel afterwards?

- How often did something similar happen to me?

- What am I fearful about while letting this anger grip me?

- Can I choose the basic emotion of love over fear? (Remember, we have only two basic emotions: love and fear).

What is basic emotion?

There are only two emotions: love and fear. All positive emotions come from love; all negative emotions come from fear.

Derivatives of love: Happiness, empathy, certainty, honour, belonging, wonder, and acceptance.

Derivatives of fear: Grief, apathy, uncertainty, shame, abandonment, horror, and anger.

You will learn more about what triggers anger by simply answering these questions. Often, you will find that it was unnecessary or there was some other better way to express yourself. However, the paucity of self-awareness in that spur of the moment created the spillover of anger.

This is how we harness curiosity to tap into our self-awareness to solve real-life issues. Better still, we can be curious about life just like children are before getting bombarded by worldly distractions and demands.

What can keep you away from self-awareness?

Now that you know the importance of self-awareness let me also share that despite knowing all these, we still do not and cannot prioritize self-awareness in our lives. There are many reasons why this happens.

Let me share some of the scenarios in which we miss out on tapping into our self-awareness:

1. When you indulge in negative self-talk.

2. By having an, 'I am my ego' mindset.

3. If you play a blame game or the victim card more often.

4. If you have an unsupportive or unrelated circle.

5. If you mainly attend to urgent (operational or symptomatic) short-term situations or issues and not looking into important (strategic or profound) long-term life aspects.

6. If you believe that fixing materialistic things first will resolve other matters quickly.

7. If your belief system is to fix external things, such as career, finance, relationships, and health, instead of working on your inner world.

Implementation Time: Increase Your Self-Awareness Trait

Create space and time and then slow down to speed up in the long term.

1. Connect with yourself daily – Prioritize having 'me-time'.

2. Avoid digital distractions – Do not be device addicted.

3. Carve out solitude – Plan and create 'mini-vacations' with yourself.

4. Practise mindfulness – Be in the NOW.

5. Pay attention to your inner state as it arises – Observe yourself non-judgementally in critical situations by pausing and delving deeper.

6. Try mindful walking, eating, and listening – Enjoy the daily activities.

7. Journal your awareness – Express your emotions, thoughts, and feelings to process them better and finally dissolve them by taking the sting out of the emotions.

8. Practise listening – Do active listening to understand others and not just respond.

9. Observe body language – Notice your body language while you speak to others.

10. Be open-minded, not judgemental – Open up your mind and heart to limitless possibilities.

11. Embrace change – Have radical acceptance. Do not resist change; the more you resist, the more you suffer.

12. Ask for feedback – Be open to feedback from others and process them impersonally.

Recommendation: I strongly recommend a self-awareness *self-assessment* – *5 Facet Mindfulness Questionnaire* where you get a personalized Mindfulness Score. Any effective self-awareness test looks at self-awareness beneath the surface. All workshop participants complete this self-assessment. In this, the Grand Mindfulness Score will give you an overall Mindfulness Score. And within that, we have five sub-areas of mindfulness that are assessed.

And within that, we have five sub-areas of mindfulness that are assessed.

* Non-react

* Non-judge

* Observative

* Describe

* Act with awareness

Scan the below QR Code and find out your mindfulness score for free.

Harness the Power of Intention – Science and Energy Perspective

In this book, I am helping you unfold who you are at your core, your passion, and what you are meant to be. At Soul In Harmony™, we have approached this quest from multiple perspectives — mindfulness, meditation, psychotherapy, subconscious mindpower, spirituality, and neuroscience.

In this section, let us understand the power of intention and the quantum theory behind conscious leadership.

If you can understand this piece, then it will be easier for you to begin in the right direction and the right spirit to cultivate conscious leadership.

An experiment by Dr. Glen Rein in 1993 revealed the effect of conscious intention on human DNA.

There were three groups of people, each holding a test tube with DNA inside. DNA was chosen because DNA is more solid, stable, and rigid than cells and bacteria.

DNA, or deoxyribonucleic acid, is the hereditary material in humans and almost all other organisms. Nearly every cell in a person's body has the same DNA.

Group 1 - Participants held the vials of DNA **with intense feelings of love, appreciation, and compassion** with no intention.

Group 2 - Participants held the vials of DNA **with the same intense feelings of love, appreciation, and compassion** as Group 1 **and also had an intention to change** the DNA.

Group 3 – In this group, participants **only intended to change DNA and had no intense feelings of love, appreciation, or compassion**.

Results:

In Group 1 and Group 3, there was zero change in DNA conformation (winding and unwinding in the DNA).

Group 2 had a remarkable 25 per cent change in DNA conformation (winding and unwinding in the DNA). They could wind and unwind the DNA structure by just thoughts, feelings, and mainly intentions.

This experiment suggests that the coherent field generated from a loving heart is insufficient to change the DNA and that a specific intention is required to direct the heart field.

Specific intentions may therefore be considered as frequency modulations of the energy fields of the heart, giving direction to these energy fields to heal a particular organ or cells.

I hope you remember the power of intention we discussed at the beginning of this book.

Through this research, Dr. Rein proves that our world, our body, and the space around us do not respond to just our wishes, wants, or intentions; Instead, it responds to two things when combined – our deep intention and intense feelings that we hold of love, appreciation, and compassion.

Nature does not give us what we 'want'; it gives us what we are 'Being'!

The data from this experiment supports the hypothesis that an energetic connection exists between structures in the quantum vacuum and corresponding structures on the physical plane and that this connection can be influenced by human intentionality.

The experimental data are also consistent with the concept that 'state of heart coherence' facilitate more significant coupling between an individual and higher dimensional (spirit-level) structures, thereby enabling human intention to interact with these structures and initiate a top-down process whereby energetic information in the quantum vacuum can be modulated and influence physical systems.

The Summary

Intentions + Emotions (either positive/negative) = Event (either positive/negative)

Know the Connection – Our Mind, Quantum Field, and Life

Let me explain how important thoughts and feelings are in a real-life scenario.

If I have thoughts such as:

1. I'll never get a job; I always fail.

2. No one ever listens to me.

3. He always makes me feel angry.

4. It's my genes; I will always struggle as my father did.

5. I cannot ever be a good leader; I have been a follower all my life.

Do not use universal quantifiers such as never, ever, no one, always, everyone, etc. These falsehoods stop you from going beyond your current reality or exploring the vast potential that we discussed above in the *Conscious Intention on Human DNA Experiment* by Dr. Rein.

Another point to remember is that your genes do not define your destiny. Epigenetics means 'above genetics,' which illustrates that something above or other than genetics, such as thoughts, belief systems, and intentions, can help alter our gene expression.

You have the power to harness the quantum field theory by feeling grateful for something that exists as a potential in the quantum field but has not yet happened in your real life.

However, there is a catch. You cannot fake the feeling in your conscious awareness. Instead, you need to suspend all the fears and doubts around this aspect that you want to project in your life – good health, an excellent loving relationship, a joyful workplace, or a successful business.

Suppose you wish for any of the optimistic scenarios mentioned but unknowingly have a belief system that negates the wish. The subconscious mind (forty million times more powerful than the conscious mind) is filled with fear, whereas the conscious mind is hooked to the positive wish.

As a result, the fear and doubt in the subconscious mind will overshadow the slight positivity and the 'empty intention' you have generated in your conscious mind.

You can move from 'Cause and Effect' to 'Causing an Effect.'

In other words, move from waiting for 'something outside you to make a change inside you' to 'change something inside you to produce an effect outside you.'

For example, if you want happiness and harmony, start being happy more often for an extended period by engaging in things that excite you, resonate with you, and keep you at an elevated consciousness. That will create happy and harmonious events in your life naturally. There are ways and means how you can do this, and I demonstrate this in my programs.

HR Department Can Leverage Self-Awareness

The establishment's Human Resources (HR) policies must be associated with organizational vision and values to realize employees' self-awareness, spiritual potential, and growth throughout their careers. Suitable intervention mechanisms for crafting 'individual role–corporate goal' fitment will create an engaging and committed workforce.

What can HR Department Do?

There are a few interventions that human resource officials can plan out. The first could be charting out mentoring relationships from the beginning of an individual's career with an experienced senior executive. This kind of initiative provides psychological safety for meaningful engagement and performance at work while making them understand the broader perspective of career and life.

HR's Proposed Value Statement

Adequate policy-level steps must be devised to enhance commitment and retention levels. The HR vision of the organization could be to realign its value statement as "only happy, engaged, emotionally intelligent employees leading a balanced life can go beyond the call of duty and walk that extra mile which is critical for realizing the vision and the company's business strategy in the long run."

Present-day organizations need to realize that the new generation of knowledge workers views their profession through the lenses of rewarding mechanisms and in terms of employee-friendly policies that can provide them with a healthy work-life balance.

84

Conclusion

There is an enormous need for self-awareness at work in engaging and retaining employees in the organization in a meaningful way. The transactional means of enticing and retaining individuals will be futile in this volatile, uncertain, complex and ambiguous (VUCA) world. Organizations must ensure that individual employees understand themselves well through mindfulness practice to boost their self-awareness levels. Then they align their purpose in life with the corporate objectives, which will help them stay committed to the organization's vision.

Remember: People do not leave bad companies; they leave bad bosses. And mind you, bad bosses often are the ones who create an unhealthy culture.

Organizations Benefit from Self-Awareness

The Missing Link

Today, most organizations are affected by an abundance of disgruntled and demotivated employees who lack a deep sense of commitment towards organizational purpose and vision. The fact remains that most employees consider work to earn a livelihood and run their families. One of the main reasons for this is that the current motivational paradigm does not incorporate a self-awareness element that adds to the consciousness dimension of employees. This missing link in the current organizational environment is the key to addressing the critical challenges around low motivation and attrition and resulting corporate under performance and ineffectiveness.

The Situation

The pressure to address workplace burnout was so heightened that in 2019 the World Health Organization (WHO) declared burnout an occupational phenomenon in the 11th Revision of the International Classification of Diseases.

According to Gallup's recent report, *Employee Burnout: Causes and Cures* 76 percent of employees experience burnout at least sometimes, and 28 percent say they are burned out "very often" or "always" at work.

A self-awareness-based conscious leadership-centred organizational culture promotes individual-organization fitment, leading to productivity and reduced employee turnover. From a human resource perspective, cultivating self-awareness (through mindfulness practice) is expected to provide a piece of solid evidence of its mission and value. In fact, with the domination of self-awareness for employees, the organization will build mutual trust and respect. It will do so by providing courage and self-confidence to the employees by letting them align their core values and strengths to the work profile by aiding self-awareness.

It is presumed that a sense of organizational citizenship behaviour is reinforced, leading to enhanced motivation and, as a result, a lower attrition rate. A research report, *Workplace Spirituality and Employee Commitment*, iterated that the concept of conscious leadership via self-awareness and workplace spirituality has now become a "major management issue" globally.

In today's VUCA (volatile, uncertain, complex, and ambiguous) world, it is tough to see employee loyalty and commitment. Organizations face considerable challenges in retaining top talent by giving them a compelling purpose beyond the typical retention methods, such as higher salaries, incentives, and perks. An individual's spiritual quest offers them that higher and clear intent to stay committed to the vision and mission of the organization.

It is speculated that the focus of the HR department in today's organization is to tap the human potential. This means commitment, a sense of belonging, confidence in management, and dedication to the job are some of the essential prerequisites to work by organizations for improving employee performance.

Employees should cultivate self-awareness to link emotionally with the organization to perform better. Hence, self-awareness has an edge in gearing up the wheels of organizational effectiveness through personal effectiveness.

In McKinsey's article *Defining the Skills Citizens Will Need in the Future World of Work*, there are 56 foundational skills across 13 skill groups and 4 categories. Self-leadership is among the four categories listed and contains more than 25 percent of the foundational skills listed.

Their research identified 56 foundational skills that will help citizens thrive in the future at work. There were 56 deltas across 13 skill groups and 4 categories.

Self-leadership is one of the four categories. It has the 3 skill groups:-

1. Self-awareness and self-management

2. Entrepreneurship

3. Goals achievement

The point to be noted here is that once an individual develops self-awareness and self-management, the other two skill groups (entrepreneurship and goals achievement) also get activated.

Conscious Leadership Stage One — Self-Awareness

Cognitive

Critical thinking	Planning and ways of working
● Structured problem solving ● Logical reasoning ● Understanding biases ● Seeking relevant information	● Work-plan development ● Time management and prioritization ● Agile thinking

Communication	Mental flexibility
● Storytelling and public speaking ● Asking the right questions ● Synthesizing messages ● Active listening	● Creativity and imagination ● Translating knowledge to different contexts ● Adopting a different perspective ● Adaptability ● Ability to learn

Interpersonal

Mobilizing systems	Developing relationships
● Role modeling ● Win–win negotiations ● Crafting an inspiring vision ● Organizational awareness	● Empathy ● Inspiring trust ● Humility ● Sociability

Teamwork effectiveness	
● Fostering inclusiveness ● Motivating different personalities ● Resolving conflicts	● Collaboration ● Coaching ● Empowering

Self-Leadership

Self-awareness and self-management	
● Understanding own emotions and triggers ● Self-control and regulation ● Understanding own strengths	● Integrity ● Self-motivation and wellness ● Self-confidence

Entrepreneurship	
● Courage and risk-taking ● Driving change and innovation	● Energy, passion, and optimism ● Breaking orthodoxies

Goals achievement	
● Ownership and decisiveness ● Achievement orientation	● Grit and persistence ● Coping with uncertainty ● Self-development

Digital

Digital fluency and citizenship	
● Digital literacy ● Digital learning	● Digital collaboration ● Digital ethics

Software use and development	
● Programming literacy ● Data analysis and statistics	● Computational and algorithmic thinking

Understanding digital systems	
● Data literacy ● Smart systems	● Cybersecurity literacy ● Tech translation and enablement

Fig. 3.1: **McKinsey & Company Research on the Future of Work – June 2021**
McKinsey & Company's research identified 56 foundational skills that will help citizens thrive in the future of work. There are 56 Foundational skills across 13 skill groups and 4 categories.

The Solution - Make Well-Being a Part of Your Culture

Conscious leadership, including mindfulness programs is causing massive improvements in workplace efficiency and happiness. With these interventions, corporates are experiencing massive reductions in employee stress and, therefore, illness and absenteeism. Employers who have adopted these programs are observing reduced attrition because they are more meaningfully engaged at work.

Ultimately, a workplace where employees can feel happy and perform their best is a win-win situation for the company, its workers, and its customers.

When well-being is on the corporate agenda, preventing and reducing burnout is imperative. In contrast, the workplace culture can brew burnout when well-being is only an HR-driven 'good-to-have' rather than the norm modelled across the organization.

This well-being culture will curb burnout and create a safe container atmosphere to foster a healthy work environment. This further fuels creativity, resilience, team culture, and performance, leading to overall corporate excellence. Most of all, these interventions can make the workplace a happy and safe space where employees thrive.

The top management can ensure regular mindfulness and conscious leadership interventions across teams and hierarchies to percolate this well-being and conscious leadership culture. There must be regular offsite retreats for both C-Suites and the rank-and-file employees to leverage the organization-wide learning and embed those values from top to bottom.

Industry Trend Regarding Conscious Leadership and Mindfulness

The five giant corporations known for their mindfulness practice are Google, General Mills, Intel, Aetna, and Goldman Sachs. Nike, Facebook, Salesforce, Apple, Pearson, and HBO are a few others.

❏

Conscious Leadership
Stage Two
Self-Reflection

According to a Zen saying, "We cannot see our reflection in running water. It is only in the still water that we can see".

Socrates famously said, "The unexamined life is not worth living."

And while this quote is undoubtedly accurate, self-reflection is not necessarily an easy thing to practise. We live in an incredibly fast-paced world. Our mobile phones are constantly buzzing, social media platforms are infinitely addictive and a part of our lives now, and OTT platforms always give us something new to binge on.

Taking the time for reflection is now a lost art. Most of us, unfortunately, are live unexamined lives.

This should not be the case. Few things seem to be more valuable than self-reflection in this rapidly-changing world.

But what exactly is self-reflection? And what are some simple ways to practise it?

Self-awareness will help you create that 'still water' environment in your life. Once you establish that, you must contemplate and deliberate about yourself and what you want from your life to have clarity and develop intentionality.

While driving home from work, Siddharth considers how the stress of his 11 am meeting that day might have led to residual frustration and a poor decision with his boss at the end of the day. As a result, Siddharth resolves, as he drives back home to pause and reflect after such stressful meetings to open up to all possibilities rather than jump right back into the next activity and react to situations and later regret them.

This is an example of how Siddharth could have saved himself from an unfortunate experience with his boss simply by self-reflecting on an incident.

Like the above, most of us are capable of self-reflection. We periodically reflect on an event and how we handled it with the hopes that we learn something from it and make better decisions in the future. We could all benefit from doing this kind of retrospective self-reflection more often. I am suggesting self-reflection, and that need not be confused with overthinking.

Note: Self-reflection becomes powerful when we can use it in real-time to make better decisions.

It is advisable to learn from past mistakes, but it is far better to catch them in the moment or try to avoid making them in the first place.

In the middle of a challenging conversation with her spouse, Shruti notices a growing sense of pride and ego, as if her mind is trying to defend her from her spouse's attack. But Shruti also harnesses her self-awareness towards her goal of getting better at just listening without justifying herself when taking feedback. As a result, she successfully resists the urge to interrupt, and she continues to listen actively and empathetically.

What did Shruti just do?

She practised self-reflection the moment the situation hit her. She could have gone impulsive on autopilot, made matters worse, and later spent more time and energy regretting it and engaging in damage control.

- How would so many failed marriages have been avoided if we had practised a little self-reflection?

- How would many high-potential businesses produce excellent results if their leaders had 10 per cent more capacity for real-time self-reflection while dealing with their teams?

- How many person-hours and dollars would organizations have saved if the HR process included self-reflection during recruitment?

Google's Recruitment Process Starts with Self-Reflection

Excerpt from Google Careers Website Section

"While we are sure you are ready to dive into the depths of the job search, we recommend starting with an often-overlooked first step: focus on yourself."

Google starts its recruitment process with the self-reflection method. This allows the candidate to align his identity and purpose with what the job offers. This well-thought-out method works for both parties – the company and the candidate.

I will share more details about this in the 5th Conscious Leadership Stage – Unified & Purposeful Growth. This is where I discuss how it is to live with a purpose and how an organization can curate a purpose-driven organization that can beat attrition and talent crunch.

You cannot build a fulfilling career on something that does not stimulate you. Therefore, Google suggests that candidates ask themselves a few questions before they apply for the job.

- What is something you learned that made everything that came after easier?

- Have more of your achievements come from solo effort or teamwork?

- What do you enjoy more, solving problems or pushing the discussion forward?

- What is the most rewarding job you have ever had? Why?

- Describe the best team you have ever worked with. What made that experience stand out?

Google does not believe in hiring based only on your skills. They are looking for a Googler with the required skills, enduring passions, unique experiences, and perspectives. And for this, they want you to go on a self-reflecting journey to create a perfect win-win.

Understand and Cultivate Self-Reflection

Simply expressed, self-reflection is taking the time to consider, meditate on, evaluate, and think seriously about your beliefs, attitudes, habits, behaviours, thoughts, choices, and actions. It is the process of diving deep into your thoughts, feelings and activities and determining the great "Why?" behind them.

Self-reflection allows you to analyse your life from a macro and micro level. At a macro level, you can evaluate the overall trajectory of your life. You can see where you are headed, determine whether you are happy with the direction, and make adjustments as necessary, for example, about your career, finances, relationships, and health.

At a micro level, you can evaluate your responses to circumstances and events, let us say, in the case of a mid-life crisis. At this level, instead of just remembering what happened, we tend to ask why it took place, what the impact was, how it could be avoided or improved, and so on. Reflection is a deeper form of learning that allows us to retain every aspect of any experience.

Practising self-reflection takes discipline and intentionality, which you know comes through self-awareness (or mindfulness practice). It requires pressing a pause on the chaos of life and simply taking the time to think and ponder about your life, which is not easy for many people because they are accustomed to living an autopilot mode of life. Therefore, self-reflection is a precious practice.

In his book *Mindsight*, Dan Siegel uses the analogy of a camera to explain self-reflection. The better the camera and clearer the lens, the more accurate the final clicked photo will be. But as any professional photographer will tell you, you must use a tripod to stabilize the camera and the lens to get the most precise image possible because even small vibrations and movements can distort the final image.

Most of us have the essential equipment for self-reflection – a decent camera and lens. But to bring our powers of self-reflection to the next level, we need to bring in the proverbial 'tripod' to cultivate three specific skills that contribute to the habit of self-reflection: **openness, observation, and objectivity**.

- **Openness** means seeing things for what they are, not what you think they should be. It means becoming aware of our biases and prejudices about the world, other people, and even ourselves and working to overcome them.

- **Observation:** It is the ability to watch yourself as a third person; watch in the same way you watch external events – with perspective and distance. This skill is beneficial for using self-reflection to overcome compulsive, addictive, or habitual behaviours.

- **Objectivity** is the ability to separate your thoughts, feelings, and behaviours from your identity and sense of self. Overthinking and over-intellectualizing are not included when we speak about objectivity. Of course, what you think, how you feel, and the behaviours you engage in are a part of who you are, but they do not completely define who you are.

Why Do You Need Self-Reflection?

Without self-reflection, we go through life without thinking, moving from one thing to the next without taking time to evaluate whether things align with our preset intention, goal, or vision. We do not pause to think and determine what is not working. Unfortunately, we often get stuck or progress on autopilot without impacting life.

For example, a lack of personal reflection may lead us to stay in a job we do not like, a business not making profits, a relationship draining us, or an unhappy marriage adding toxicity to life.

With self-reflection, we can take corrective actions to mend it or make a mindful exit without future regrets.

A lack of reflection causes us to keep running, trying to keep up with things and put up a false positive outlook despite things not working out. We do the same things repeatedly, even if those things are not producing the expected outcomes.

Let us acknowledge and honour the fact: Taking time for self-reflection can be difficult. It can be challenging to take the necessary time to pause, step back and reflect on what truly matters. However, with the earlier stage of self-awareness, you will know when to pause for self-reflection. There are numerous beautiful benefits of self-reflection, and we should prioritize it.

1. Allows you to gain perspective

Emotions can cloud your judgement, and you can lose sight of what truly matters to you. Some things are assumed as per our biases, prejudices, or past experiences. This is how reality shifts and situations seem worse than they are.

Self-reflection allows you to take a step back and gain perspective on what you must stand for and what you can let go of. It will enable you to process events as they are and not as they should be and finally achieve clarity.

2. Helps you to respond more effectively

As explained above, we are better positioned to respond to circumstances when we see things as they are. We can avoid being impulsive and do things that take more time, effort, and energy to mend later on, and it only leaves us with lifelong regret. When we are in a reactive mode, we do not take the necessary time to consider our actions and words.

Personal reflection allows you to consider the consequences of your words and actions. It also lets you respond in the best, most effective and most helpful manner in a given situation.

3. Promotes learning and understanding

When we go through life without pausing to think and reflect, we do not allow ourselves to learn or gain a deeper understanding of the things happening around us. We simply move from one thing to the next, never pausing to consider what valuable lessons we might learn. This is precisely what happened to me when I switched from one job to another in search of a more significant role and a pay cheque but never evaluated where my strengths, gifts, and talents lay.

Self-reflection, on the other hand, enables us to evaluate and process what we have experienced. It allows us to think deeply, ponder our circumstances' meaning, and integrate the lessons to live holistic, integrated, and fulfilling lives.

Take Three Concrete Steps to Successful Self-Reflection

1. Identify the "what" of self-reflection

Once you feel the calmness inside, direct your focus inward. Choose a specific matter or life situation you want to change. Pull up a memory of a critical incident related to that life episode.

- What impressions arise as you focus on this issue?

- What does it make you feel?

- What does it make you think?

2. Identify the "why" of self-reflection

With your mind quiet when you have shortlisted the one significant thing that you wish to change, try to look deeper. Aim to go to the most critical aspects of the above issue.

- What did you feel, think, or do?

  Now, go a layer deeper, and ask yourself.

- Why did you think, feel, or do these things?

  This kind of inner search-and-discovery with self-reflection can reveal something buried deep down and might be, at times, scary, so go at your own pace. Always be kind to yourself as you learn more about what is underneath. Do not judge or self-beat; just acknowledge with a feeling of gratitude that you are capable of doing this process.

3. Use self-reflection as a tool for change

Why do we self-reflect?

Because we want to change something about our past and the next step is cultivating the desire to change behaviours that bother us.

After identifying any problematic aspects of yourself, take baby steps and slowly shift your behaviour in ways that better represent:

- How you want to be

- The life you want to live

- The career you want to have

- The relationships you want to nurture

Note: Recall the "The 3 Circles Approach to Avoid Overthinking" discussed earlier in this book. Self-reflection is not to be confused with overthinking.

If you thought "that issue" was "resolved," but it still keeps coming back, self-reflect once again to check if you missed something essential or were unconsciously hiding something from yourself. It is challenging to change ourselves or our behaviour, and it may take several attempts to resolve the issue thoroughly, so accept and appreciate yourself for trying.

Know the Key Outcome of Self-Reflection

When you self-reflect, **you see a different reality with your self-awareness.** You are bound to observe your true worth. And one of the results of this realization is that you will reprioritize and find it harder to stay around the same people or situation, causing repeated concern. Therefore, do not sulk in self-doubt. There is something else going on at a deeper level, and as a result, you drift away from some people. Let me explain this further.

Everything is energy, and energy is everything. Even though you and I are flesh, bones, and blood, deep within, we are all atoms and molecules. Ultimately these atoms and molecules have wave patterns. Our thoughts are also waves. So, your thoughts are waves in another plane of existence. As you are aware, waves transmit, and so do our thoughts, which are essentially energy.

When we get into the transformation journey, our self-awareness is heightened first. Then our belief systems get rewritten positively, and we start behaving and acting differently. Our thoughts transform, which transmits to those close to us.

Earlier, you both resonated with each other, but now your energy has shifted, so there is either no or less resonance. Congratulations on making it here! You are a brave one and have crossed a significant milestone. You both cannot relate to each other anymore. Do not sulk in this solitude; instead, be delighted.

The reason, my friend, is that you have transformed, which is a "good problem". With the same logic, you will also attract like-minded soulful people who will help you progress to the next level of your growth journey. This new association will serve you on your new growth path, not the earlier set of people who could not relate to your new version. It is prudent not to

103

spare time and energy analysing and self-doubting; instead, acknowledge the rare milestone you have achieved and allow yourself to keep the flame of personal growth burning. That is how you evolve through change and allow yourself to transform from a caterpillar to a butterfly.

❏

Conscious Leadership
Stage Three
Acceptance and Forgiveness

*"To forgive is to set a prisoner free and discover
that the prisoner was you."*

– Lewis Smedes

*"Forgiveness does not change the past,
but it does enlarge the future."*

– Paul Boose

This stage is often very tricky. There are two reasons for the same:

1. It may be skipped because you might think it is insignificant; therefore, there is not much to ponder.

2. Secondly, we all believe that we are correct and that our behaviours are justified. We have enough excuses not to forgive others and ourselves too. Yes, you read it right!

You need to look at forgiveness by applying it to others and yourself. I will discuss forgiving yourself later. Let us discuss forgiving others first.

We tell people we have forgiven them all the time, but the truth is, in most cases, we have not done so. Suppose you have forgiven a colleague but harbour resentment and a memory of how badly they treated you. In that case, you are hanging on to a harsh judgement about that individual; you are bringing the past into the present, re-investing in your victimhood, and, therefore, you have not forgiven them.

Practicing Forgiveness and Acceptance is Not an Option – You Must!

- **Medical evidence:** Studies have proven that long-held resentment is toxic and damages our physical and emotional well-being. Gautam Buddha said – holding on to anger and resentment is like drinking poison and expecting the other person to die.

- **Take charge of your life:** Stop giving yourself an excuse for not forgiving. Take control of your life. That does not mean that you do not have legitimate reasons to have anger towards a person. Also, at times others could victimize us. However, remaining a victim by clinging to the past is a choice we can make.

- **Forgiveness is freedom:** Forgiving someone is akin to cutting the invisible cords that bind you to the person who hurt you – think of it as taking back the remote control of your life that you had given to someone else until now. You are restoring your balance by releasing the resentment and pent-up emotions that may be stuck inside your body, mind, and heart.

- **Focus on a new purpose:** Redirect your energy and focus on a new purpose. You feel lighter because of your energy and your mindset shift. You can then think of doing things that were once impossible. Your intuition and inspiration are heightened because you are no more biased or looking through tinted glasses. The scene is set for a new beginning.

- **Forgiveness allows your life to flow more freely:** Just as the kitchen sink is clogged with food scraps and stops the flow of water, jamming the whole system, anger and resentment block the flow of free energy and make our view of life so clouded and painful. Forgiveness removes the unwanted debris of negative energy to create space for positive possibilities.

I hope you remember the formula, $P * R = S$

Where P = Pain, R = Resistance and S = Suffering

Pain is fixed for all individuals (as it refers to an individual's threshold), and resistance is the only variable.

Therefore, more the resistance, more the suffering! Have more acceptance in life and move ahead with forgiveness.

Leverage the Secret Sauce of Conscious Leadership

The fear of forgiving is what holds us back. But why do we dread forgiveness?

Part of the fear of forgiving other people is that we think we will become punching bags, weaklings, and people will walk all over us. But we need to forgive with compassion and understanding, keeping the idea of self-care at the centre. We also need to be fully aware that we do not allow this situation to repeat and avoid being complacent about what has happened.

Genuine forgiveness means no harmful residue left in our minds and heart.

We do not wish them ill; we only want what is best for them – even if we never see them again. And for us, forgiveness does not mean a lack of conscience. Just the opposite, forgiveness makes us more conscious of our actions and increases our capacity for compassion and kindness. It opens our hearts, and we are far less likely to hurt anyone, including ourselves, when our hearts are open.

Acceptance and Forgiveness is the secret sauce of conscious leadership.

This is one of the most critical aspects of the conscious-leadership framework. Reconciling differences between yourself and others is vital. It needs self-awareness and self-reflection. If you go through stages one and two of conscious leadership and fail at this stage three, then however hard you attempt your personal growth, it will not go beyond a point. That is why you may consider forgiveness and acceptance **a secret sauce of conscious leadership. Only after this stage is resolved will you be able**

to lead forward. Else, you can keep circling back in the same conundrum of self-awareness and self-reflection.

You might have met people who are observant and passionate about personal growth. They read books, attend many seminars and workshops, and follow rituals. However, they somehow keep circling back to the same negative life situation. I have found out that most of the time, forgiveness and acceptance are missing.

During my workshops and retreats, I have often spotted that the individuals who adopt forgiveness and embrace acceptance in their approach see a quantum jump in their growth journey. The reason is – forgiveness opens your heart *chakra (Anahata Chakra)*. Being consciously passionate about self-improvement and having no associated emotions is the same as telling yourself, "I can live with my head, and I do not need a heart!"

However, if you follow forgiveness with a clear conscience and complete intention, you mindfully include the heart in this paradigm of personal growth. Consequently, you can expect sudden changes in your inner world that will inadvertently affect your outer world positively.

My participants had massive shifts in their awareness levels in my mindfulness programs, conscious leadership workshops and retreats. Later, they confessed to managing their thoughts, writing affirmations, maintaining a vision board and creating a positive world with almost no results. And as soon as they included this forgiveness element, things started shifting magically. New options opened and unleashed massive transformations.

There are two main aspects of forgiveness and acceptance, and it is essential to know that.

Two Main Aspects of Forgiveness and Acceptance

1. **Forgive and accept ourselves first:** We need to acknowledge that we have hurt others, knowingly or unknowingly and that we did it because we were driven by confusion, fear, desire, jealousy, or hatred. It is not easy to look at our mistakes, primarily when our actions have caused harm to others.

   Forgiving ourselves is hard. That is where we are vulnerable, exposed, and raw. It embarrasses us to look at some of the things we have done. None of us want to admit we have caused pain, but if we cannot accept it, we cannot forgive it either. We are humans, and we can err. Every human being would have behaved erroneously at some time or another. But we also hold the option of forgiving ourselves for doing so. We need to exercise that choice and not indulge in giving lame excuses to ourselves or feel embarrassed.

   We need to forgive ourselves for removing the roots of guilt and shame so that we can go up towards love, joy, and peace on the **Hawkins Scale of Consciousness (discussed in the section – Pump Up Your Life Energetically).**

2. **Forgive others:** After you have forgiven yourself is the time when you are prepared to forgive others. If you have genuinely forgiven yourself, how can you not forgive others? Because now you know that others can also make the mistakes and blunders you have made.

   In reality, this is easier said than done. I have seen cases where a conscious practitioner of personal growth has forgiven himself and most others but is stuck with one person. His conscience doesn't allow him to forgive that one specific individual. In most cases, I have found debris of intense feelings for relationships (spouses, ex-business partners, estranged siblings) who cheated

111

or mistreated them. As a result, they lose their self-esteem and trust in other people.

Forgiving others yet having non-acceptance of a particular situation is possible. As explained above about the debris of intense feelings, it might be the last and final bastion to be won to become joyful and abundant again. The typical cases that pose challenges are divorce, break-ups from a long-term relationship, a cheating case, or a breach of trust with close relatives or a business partner who was instrumental in altering the life trajectory of the person in question.

You will not be punished for your anger; you will be punished by your anger.

Four Things to Remember While Forgiving

- Forgiving does not mean you need to forget the lesson implied or wrapped in that incident.

- Forgiving is more about buying your peace than concluding who was wrong.

- Forgiving is not a social cause directed at the other person – it is about you and is meant to heal and progress or facilitate your true success, harmony, and joy that is rightfully yours.

- By forgiveness and acceptance, you take control of yourself so that you control the buttons of your life.

❑

RE-SCULPT
Stage Four
(Revamp Self-Image, Unified & Purposeful Growth)

RE-SCULPT
Stage Four
(Revamp Self-Image, Unified & Purposeful Growth)

Conscious Leadership Stage Four - Revamp Self-Image

"You are confined only by the walls you build yourself."

– Andrew Murphy

"No one is you, and that's your superpower!"

– Anonymous

Replace Your Shadow Side – Scientific Perspective

Your self-image is the most crucial part when you observe yourself inside out. A lot depends on your self-image if you aim to create true success, lasting happiness and inner peace in your life. It will not be wrong to say that your self-image will be a significant stumbling block when you want to transform your life. This is where you will typically get stuck and keep going around in circles by failing at whatever goals you set for yourself. Now you might wonder what is so detrimental about this self-image regarding life transformation.

When you see who you have been so far and why your life was behaving in a specific way, you become aware of the need to address your negative self-image. That is because you need to remove or sweep the dust from under the carpet that was lying there and accumulating over the years. Well, that dust under the rug is nothing but the negative self-image that you had created. This realization is what leads you to reprogram your mind.

Dr. Maxwell Maltz, the author of the world-renowned book *Psycho-Cybernetics* and a cosmetic surgeon, found that cosmetic plastic surgery did not only affect the physical appearance of someone but produced deep incisions into the human psyche.

He inferred that something at the core of our minds determines how we see ourselves, regardless of the objective reality, and thus how we feel and behave. This is called the "self-image." The self-image is our conception of the "kind of person we are"; it is the mental model we have unknowingly created over the years.

The key is that your actions, feelings, behaviours, and abilities are always consistent with this self-image. In short, you will "act like" the person you conceive yourself to be. Not

115

only this, but you literally cannot act otherwise, despite all your conscious efforts or will power. This is the genesis of the mental reprogramming of the negative self-image.

Create on Your Own – You are Not Your Genes

Dr. Bruce Lipton, a globally acclaimed stem cell biologist and best-selling author, proved through an experiment that our environment and visualization primarily defines us, not our genes.

In an experiment, he divided 30,000 genetically identical cells into three parts from the same parent cell. He split those into three Petri dishes. Then, he grew the cells in a culture medium, the lab equivalent of human blood, for experiment purposes.

Here is the exciting thing; he developed three different compositions of culture medium – Culture medium A, Culture medium B, and Culture medium C.

Dr. Lipton then fed dish 1 with culture medium A, dish 2 with culture medium B, and dish 3 with culture medium C.

In a few weeks, in dish 1, the cells formed bones; in dish 2, the cells formed muscles; in dish 3, the cells turned to fat mass.

Why did the identical cells from the same parent cell grow differently?

This result was profound because he realized that genes do not decide the cells' fate. All the cells were from the same parent cell having the same genetics. But how can one culture medium have muscle while others have bone and fat?

And culture medium is the environment of the cells.

Therefore, the culture medium (cells' environment) was the deciding factor for the identical cells' growth. He then concluded that genes respond to the culture medium (the environment of the cells).

Dr. Lipton concluded from this experiment that an average human body has almost 50 trillion cells, and the genes do not decide our health or disease. Instead, the blood (the environment for our cells) determines our well-being.

So, genetic control is not in the genes but in the blood.

Then comes an important question for us – who is the chemist of the blood in our body?

The answer is – The brain!

Our brain releases the chemistry into the blood to control the fate of the cells!

The final and the most vital question is – what decides the chemistry in the brain?

The answer is – The Picture in the Mind!

So, if you have a picture of health, happiness and success in your mind, you have good blood chemistry. And vice versa is also true.

So, what we visualize (the picture in our mind) is how we become. This shows how powerful the images that we hold in our minds are.

The mind sees a picture of whatever we think or imagine. After that, it releases the chemistry, which affects the blood and finally plays a role in our health or disease. So, visualization plays a crucial and seminal role in our lives. What we imagine and what stories we tell ourselves ultimately shapes our life.

The picture that your mind fetches while thinking is always in sync with the self-image that you have created for yourself. Dr. Maxwell Maltz communicated this through his experience dealing with cosmetic surgery patients. Most of the time, the patients' self-image changed after the surgery, and they became incredibly successful.

Your Chance to Re-Sculpt Your Self-Image

There are various ways to re-engineer our self-image, and one of the most effective ways is a mindfulness practice or regular meditation. Mindfulness practice and meditation are two different things. One big difference is – Mindfulness can be practised formally or informally. Both mindfulness and meditation are sure-shot ways to cultivate your self-awareness and remove the biases and acquired negative belief systems. Both can help you to show your authentic self to the world with fearlessness.

This is precisely why all my workshops, programs, and retreats highlight the importance of mindfulness and meditation. These are very organic and unforced methods without any side effects that you can try over a period. Remember, patience and consistency are the keys. Do not get into the trap of shortcuts while working on your self-image. There are a few costly, unnatural options with possible adverse side effects and no guarantee. Please do not give in to these options to work on your self-image.

You need to generate happy hormones such as dopamine, oxytocin, serotonin, and endorphin through your practices and rituals while working on your self-image. It would help if you felt at ease as you worked on yourself. Cortisol does the opposite in your body. Cortisol is generated when you undergo stress, and you need to be mindful of not causing stress at any point in your growth practices. When you are too engrossed in the outcome and are not in the present moment, you are in the 'doing mode' instead of 'being mode.'

Mindfulness Comes to Your Rescue Again

Creating a new self-image in the 'doing mode' is impossible. Understand this – if we are not enjoying the process, we are

119

simply intellectualizing and mechanizing the activity. You are simply working at your conscious mind level, and your subconscious mind is not being addressed as it should have been to reveal, relive and release the unwanted memories and belief systems.

Not to forget that to live life and visualize in the right way moment-to-moment, you need self-awareness. If you are not self-aware, you drift into the normal brain mode, which is naturally tuned to negativity because of the negativity bias that our brain has.

Our brain has evolved over millions of years to keep us safe and keeps scanning for warning signs like a radar. Thanks to our brain's negative bias, which has defined many neutral events as avoidable. Our negatively charged subconscious mind then tries hard to persuade us to avoid those life experiences. Consequently, we start imagining negative scenarios for something that might otherwise be safe.

For example, if you were asked to speak during your colleague's send-off or farewell party and you fumbled for words and said something that was not as per your expectation because you were thinking about your father who was hospitalized. In fact, just after this party, you had to rush to that hospital.

The next time your manager nominates you to deliver a client presentation, you are unwilling to accept as an opportunity. The reason is that your mind already has evidence of a failure in a similar public speaking situation. The jitters or nervousness you experience for upcoming events result from negative self-talk from the previous incident at the send-off party.

You can solve this problem with a mindfulness practice that will enable you to look at events and situations objectively and not with biases due to bad experiences. So, you must master mindfulness moment-to-moment to avoid getting into a negative brain trap and break free from the negative self-image already created.

Achieve Positive Visualization Despite the Negative Happenings

Step 1: Pick up one negative programme you wish to change

To make the matter simple, we need to **pick up one negative programming at a time that we need to change**.

Our mind is Teflon for good and Velcro for bad – which means it will keep checking for proof that aligns with your negative programming. During my growing up years, my negative programming was – 'I am not good enough!' My negative programming – 'I am not good enough' used to search for evidence of real-life situations where I felt I was not good enough.

When I was invited to any birthday parties, I would enter the room and, for the time being, stand in one corner to become comfortable. Immediately my mind would echo to me – 'See, no one is with you; you like being with yourself always. Maybe people find you odd because you are not good enough.'

This is not an accurate interpretation, however. The fact is that I just let the negative bias of my mind build a negative story for a neutral situation. This happens because the mind tries to provide evidence for the negative programming or self-image we have installed. Then your mind will shout again, "I knew you were like this; it is proven again today."

And this is how the root of your negative programming keeps becoming stronger. This is how the negative self-image gets reinforced.

Step 2: Search and reflect on an incident on the opposite polarity

Now think of an incident opposite to the chosen negative programming you want to change.

If you want to work on your 'I am not good enough' self-image, then try to recollect incidents from your life where you received accolades for your exemplary achievement that proves that you were shining in life due to what you did and your self-confidence was high.

You can pick up one negative programme at a time and visualize a positive event opposite to that or journal two–three positive events in your physical or digital notebook. Start documenting your positive proofs in your journal, no matter how small, but the consistency will take you through. You need to jot down every minor piece of evidence, and if you do not find them easily, dig deeper, they are very much there. Open your heart and mind.

When I was low on confidence in my school days, I unknowingly started to participate more in sports and games and realized that I simply went into a flow state while engaging in any sporting activity. And I discovered that I was incredible in most of the sporting activities I participated in.

I bagged all four championships available to the senior category that year – Individual Championship, Dash Championship, Long Distance Championship, and Sportsman of the Year Championship. I was also the torchbearer of my School Sports Day for that year. Finally, I was the House Captain of the winning house that year. This year's sports day is etched in my memory very vividly.

This positive real-life evidence helped me overwrite my negative programming — I am not good enough.

I visualized the details of these sports day accomplishments to enhance and reinforce my positive self-image against the old negative self-image – I am not good enough. It created an enormous amount of positive ripple effects in my childhood. And reflecting on these positive incidents caused another set of positive events as I was growing up. Now I have a vast collection of positive programming, which helps me hold on to a positive self-image most of the time.

I started my one-to-one Intuitive Life Coaching session long ago and took my hesitant baby steps towards doing more such sessions. I have done almost five thousand one-on-one sessions in the last ten years, and then I did corporate and public workshops, events, programs, and keynote speeches and impacted more than forty-five thousand lives across ten nations. So, every minuscule step matters. But it needs to be consistent with an eye on the negatively biased brain and ensure it does not sabotage growth.

The negative self-image — 'I am not good enough' got overwritten with my positive self-image of confidence and grit. It took me time to overwrite that negativity, but it was permanently flushed out with a lot of self-awareness, consistency and intentionality. You can do the same to overwrite your negative programming.

Reframe Your Negative Self-Image

By visualizing and running through positive real-life images against the negatively held self-image, you will be able to give enough positive evidence to the brain to prime itself on the positive side. And I have no doubts that you also have many positive incidents in your life that you can use as evidence to overwrite the negative biases you wish to remove.

You need to use self-awareness to bring the unwanted subconscious biases to the surface of your conscious mind, work on them with positive evidence consciously, and repeat this process multiple times to transform your negative tendencies into positive ones with the help of visualizing the real-life evidence.

This will change your self-image, personality, identity, and, more essentially, the stories you regale yourself with every moment.

So, you can keep transforming the negative biases of your mind. As I said, the mind is Teflon for good and Velcro for bad. So, you must be conscious doorkeepers to your mind and keep a strict vigil on what we allow inside it.

Reframe Your Negative Self-Image – Illustration
Positive Programming Daily Activity

(A five-minute activity)

- What area of your life that you want to boost?

- Mention at least three positive proofs from your life for this category (moments where you were in your best form).

Now, this is the habit that you need to start today. Every day, you need to make a note of three positive proofs from your life in the area you want to work upon. Some days if it is hard to find three positive incidents, you may repeat them with no issues. However, try and excavate new pieces of evidence from your past. If you fail to get all three new, you might repeat.

This is how we train the mind to start acknowledging the positives of our life against getting sucked into the negative side on autopilot.

This will help to cultivate positive habits, behaviour, attitude, and finally, a belief system with your conscious self-awareness.

How does the identity gap form?

The negative programming creates a negative self-image, creating a shadow side in the brain. This shadow side results in an identity gap that is visible to others. By now, you know well that these programs are created as we encounter different life situations and environments as we progress in life. Consequently, there is an identity gap. This identity gap is a critical concern; if we can resolve this, we have sorted out the self-image by addressing the shadow side.

Discover Your Identity Gap to Bridge It

The identity gap is the difference between 'how we appear to the world' and 'who we are inside'.

'How we appear to the world' comprises the following elements:

1. The identity I project to the outer environment.

2. What do I want you to think I am.

3. The façade I wish to project.

   This is mostly 'ideal' for the world.

   'Who we are inside' comprises the following elements:

1. How do I feel?

2. Who am I?

3. How am I on the inside?

   This is mostly 'ideal' for self.

   What separates 'how we appear to the world' from 'who we are inside'?

   The layers of emotions that separate the two are as follows:

- Unworthiness

- Anger

- Fear

- Shame

- Self-doubt

- Guilt

Since childhood, our minds have got tattooed with emotionally charged events. We relive these events repeatedly and keep them running inside emotionally for a long time till we realize the menace that the adverse events can create if we do not stop them. Permitting to run these damaging event programs is doing more harm than good.

The emotional events create mind tattoos. These mind tattoos design our temperament. This temperament forges our personality traits. The personality trait finally sculpts our self-image. Notice that it all started from the emotional event experience.

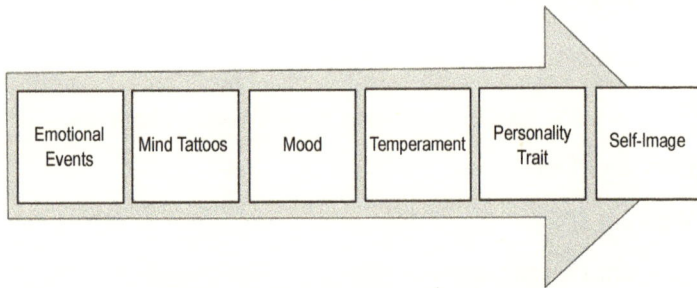

Fig. 4.1: ***Stages of Self-Image Creation***
How Emotional events lead to self-image creation through various stages.

I was just back home from my Latin American trip while in IBM's Marketing Centre of Excellence Team. I was sitting on my couch at home in the weekend and was thinking about what it means to be happy. I contemplated my lack of fulfilment and joy. I imagined telling myself something like this verbatim: *You are fortunate. You have a job, you dreamt of during your MBA campus placement days; you have a wonderful family (my wife was pregnant then). You are a successful marketing professional working for a fifth-ranked Fortune 500 company in a senior marketing role with a promising career. You get to work with global stakeholders and travel to work with them directly. You have a Tier1 UK visa in hand, which means you are just*

128

one step away from living and working in the UK in a global marketing role. You were a part of the leadership team in the Global Marketing Centre with exposure to global work culture. (I had the option of growing inside the India Global Marketing team or migrating to the UK for a different kind of life). You are so well placed in your career in just ten years!

It would have been a perfect career graph for any sales and marketing professional, but something was not right for me!

I was at a point in my life where I was swamped while ramping up my career graph, working smart, making connections, and attending networking events and conferences. I did not even have time to pause and wonder if I was being honest with myself, whether I was living a life true to myself or based on something others expected of me.

This was disturbing because I realized that all the happiness I had created for myself was based on external validation. In contrast, my travel, networking, and leadership role had nothing to do with joy. I was projecting an image of myself that was dependent on external forces. And when I was not working or was not in any event, conference, or client presentation, I felt an emptiness and void.

In no sense of the word, I am disregarding the achievements I had secured and speaking against having them; it is fantastic to have achievements and accolades. But the sad truth is that while I seemed happy on the outside due to these achievements. However, if you would have asked me during one of those moments, I would have probably responded – "Yes, I am a fortunate person, and I am doing well, and things are going successfully for me."

But suppose you had caught me in a quiet moment. When I was away from all the activities, I would respond in a perplexed and different manner, saying, "Something is missing. I feel incomplete and unsettled. Things are not that exciting, and I need to add some authentic flavour into my life."

That day I realized the innate reason for my unhappiness. I realized that I wanted the external world to see me in a certain way and accept me as a successful person. I liked the world to remember who I was in terms of the job I held, the house I lived in, the car I drove, the countries I travelled to, the team size I handled and the experiences I needed to reaffirm myself as this person named Sandiip Panndit.

And when I was not in a working environment with my colleagues who could help me recall this personality that the world might know me as, I was not sure of my identity anymore. I understood that all my perceived happiness was in reaction to the environment and that I was deeply addicted to my environment. I was utterly dependent on external cues to reinforce my emotional addiction to my outward identity.

What a moment that was for me! I had read and heard from wise people a million times that happiness comes from within, but I was simply happy with the autopilot life I was leading, looking outwards.

As I sat on my couch in my house that Sunday afternoon, I looked out of the window and saw an image. I envisioned myself on the stage delivering a life-transforming speech to the audience, all dressed formally. I was intrigued by this because, in childhood, the stage moments had changed my personality trajectory, and now again! This was like a *deja-vu* moment, but I could not arrive at anything concrete on that day.

Mid-Life Crisis Can Jolt You

The event-based deep emotions from childhood stay hidden for a long time because we are busy preparing ourselves for life by studying, doing professional courses, acquiring new skills, having new experiences like friendships, marriage, buying houses, having children, and so on. And all these new experiences have emotions that hide those feelings that we had from our childhood events. We do many things in the external world to define our identity. This distracts us from how we truly feel inside.

We continue this way for a few years to accomplish many things our society expects us to achieve. We go outside our comfort zones and go beyond those real deep feelings that once defined us.

But it will always catch up with us when we do not overcome our limitations and continue to carry our baggage from our past. This happens mainly around the mid-30s (it can vary significantly from one person to another, and you can expect a mid-life crisis even till the mid-50s).

When we reach mid-life, nothing can take away that feeling of emptiness for most of us. You wake up in the morning feeling the same person. Those external environments you relied on so heavily to mask your pain, guilt, or suffering are no longer capable of removing those feelings. You feel like a leopard, which cannot change its spots. This is the mid-life crisis. Some of us still try hard to keep those feelings buried.

They buy a new sports car, own a mansion, go on a world tour, or join a new elite social club to meet new people. Some others remodel their homes, and so on.

But when the mid-life crisis hits you, you realize — What matters is 'who you are' and not 'how you appear'.

131

The Identity Gap Creates Misery

The gap between 'how we appear to the world' and 'who we are inside' is what creates misery for us. It requires infinite vulnerability to collapse or reduce the gap as much as possible. And let me tell you that vulnerability is a sign of inner strength. The one with self-awareness and clarity can tap into it and attempt to bridge this gap, but many individuals need to work on themselves. Unfortunately, they are unaware of this gap, and therefore there is no way they can do anything about it. I call it a pathetic slumber. To come out of this slumber, we need to live authentically, conquer ourselves or get people to accept us for who we are. This 'closing the gap' must begin from within.

Suppose you had an incident 20 years ago where you felt like an insecure or weak person and stopped growing emotionally two decades ago. You were busy hiding that image through external transactions, which did not help you eliminate that buried insecurity. And if a similar experience shows up in your present life, that event will trigger the same emotions, and you will act like that person did twenty years ago.

So, in a way, your soul is speaking to you – "Pay attention; I'm letting you know that nothing is bringing you joy. If you keep playing this game, I will stop trying to wake you up, and you will go back to deep sleep. Then I will see you when your life is over."

Yet, most of us change often only when faced with a crisis or trauma.

Let me share some examples of traumas.

Physical trauma – accident, chronic illness.

Emotional trauma – the loss of a loved one (family, love, close friend).

Spiritual trauma – a series of deep setbacks which makes us wonder how the world operates.

Financial trauma – Job loss, bankruptcy in business, cheating, fraud.

All the above is about losing something. So, why wait for trauma or loss due to the negative emotional state?

We have two options to work on our negative self-image.

- Learn and change in crisis and trauma (reactive approach).

- Learn and change in a state of joy and inspiration (proactive approach).

Let us be wise here and choose the second proactive option!

Closing the Gap – Waking Up from Slumber

There are two steps to close this gap between 'how we appear to the world' and 'who we are inside'.

Step 1 : Unmemorize the emotions

Step 2 : Liberating these emotional energies to transform your emotion into wisdom

Remember: A memory without emotion is called wisdom.

It is like going into the operating system of your subconscious mind, bringing all the hidden harmful data into your conscious awareness, and seeing where these critical data controlling your life are located. Then you become aware of your unconscious self.

Another way you can visualize this is – Imagine that you have outstretched both your arms to push the opposite walls of your room while standing. Do you imagine how much energy you are consumed by trying to keep those two opposite walls from crushing you? Instead of trying to hold the two walls in their place, imagine if you released those two walls, took a few steps forward and walked out of that room, and entered a completely new one.

And in the room behind you, the walls come together so that you cannot get back to it. We need to 'unmemorize' the emotions and replace them with something new.

Activity to Unmemorize Negative Emotions:

1. List your weaker areas, limiting beliefs, and negative emotions you notice.

2. Also, list the strong areas and identify your empowering beliefs or programs that hold those empowering beliefs.

3. Try reaching the source of those limiting beliefs from step one and going back to past experiences (mostly childhood or adolescence).

4. Write down the ideal beliefs and programs from step three that you want to replace the limiting beliefs identified in step one.

This will be an ongoing process of spotting, uprooting and replacing from now onwards. This requires you to bring a few subconscious habits to the conscious level and then tackle it objectively without any analysis.

Additional suggested practices: meditation, mindfulness practice, journaling and alpha affirmation meditation. We conduct live programs and also have on-demand courses which incorporate this. One of the top on-demand programs, endorsed by John Mattone (the world's Top Leadership Coach), is Self-Mastery Code.

This way, you can re-write the positive programs of your choice over the negative ones you wish to flush out from your life. In the next chapter, I will share how I revamped my self-image to craft new possibilities and a wider horizon.

If You Are Going Through Hell, Keep Going

My Personal Transformation Story

Winston Churchill said, "If you are going through hell, keep going."

The path to transformation is challenging, but when you are transformed, the grind you go through will be well worth the effort.

Earlier in this chapter, I explained to you the moment when I was sitting on my couch and realized there was a big gap between who I was and the identity I projected to the world. I will end this chapter by telling you the rest of the story. Around this time, I was actively involved in global marketing projects with stakeholders across Europe and Latin America. I felt alive at meetings and conferences, and people would find me happy. But at that moment, on the couch, I was numbed. That is when it dawned on me that I had started believing I was somebody else just to fit myself retrospectively into society's definition of success. But I had forgotten to look at joyfulness and fulfilment in their complete form.

As I sat that Sunday afternoon, I felt my heart pounding and my breath letting my belly rise and fall. I realized instantly that this cosmic intelligence is a part of my existence that knows everything. I had disconnected myself from that intelligence. I closed my eyes and let my awareness scan through my true being. I started to admit who I had been, what I had been hiding, and how unhappy I was. After this confession to myself, I began to surrender and let go of some rigidly held self-beliefs and allowed my greater mind, inner core, or my actual existence to take over and guide me intuitively.

I reminded myself of who I no longer wanted to be and decided how I wanted to give up my old personality. Next, I observed my subconscious belief systems, attitude, behaviours, thoughts, and feelings that fuelled my old self and reviewed them till they came to my conscious awareness.

Then, I thought about who I wanted to be as a new personality till I started to feel myself in that new avatar by visualizing that state of mind vividly; I became that new person! Suddenly, I felt a rush of joy right through my body, just like I felt while crossing the finishing line during a race. I knew that I was onto something profound.

I closed my eyes and let myself slow down in all ways, becoming aware of my heartbeat and conscious awareness. I lost touch with the outside world and was connected to my deeper existence. This new identity was completely free from any external forces.

I envisioned bringing transformation to others' lives by honing my gifts and talents since childhood to help others who wish to transcend the limitations our environment imposes on us.

It was a positive and joyful experience to notice myself full of vitality, vigour, and a sense of victory. All the masks wore were removed, and I wanted to get more clarity about this new identity I had discovered from the depth of my core existence.

So, I slowed down from the corporate hustle and bustle and shifted to other roles and jobs in the next one to two years to allow my natural flow of life to take over. I gave up a promotion opportunity, discarded migrating to the UK as an option, and started meditating more often and regularly. I ritualized my life to a great extent and stopped being in the auto-pilot mode of living.

This regular practice allowed my conscious awareness to notice what my innate intelligence was pointing me towards. Many serendipities started taking place. I got to attend appropriate workshops, seminars, and conferences that helped me rediscover myself. I got my hands on the exact books I was meant to read and connected with the right people's life stories which fuelled my desire to become the real me.

I was deeply moved and influenced by Dr. Wayne Dyer's work and Oprah Winfrey's life. Sadhguru's explanations about life events helped me put a perspective on these inner changes from a practical standpoint.

I attended programs my heart wished for and spent a lot of time and money on my self-education. In hindsight, I feel these were investments, not expenses, to reclaim my hidden identity and live a life true to myself.

I started coaching corporate professionals with the realizations, learnings, and experiences I had during my journey of connecting back to who I was and to my core values of freedom, authenticity, and personal growth. The sessions went exceptionally well, and I felt so joyful seeing the glint in their eyes and the confidence in their attitude after I helped them connect to their purpose and meaning in life. While supporting corporate professionals to gain meaning in life, I also earned my sense of meaning and purpose. So, this was a sure win-win. I knew this was the path I must continue treading.

A point came when I was prepared to sacrifice almost anything and move ahead of my corporate career to pursue life transformation services for those willing to live a fulfilling and meaningful life. This career in India was way ahead of its time in 2014. However, I started practising in 2010 but decided to take a leap of faith in making it full-time four years later when I saw client success stories emerging from ten countries.

I was no longer living for the ideal world but was living from the standpoint of serving people based on the gifts and talents I was endowed with when I was born. This purpose was safely and carefully placed in my heart; after discovering it, there was no way I could have let it lose its shine. There were distractions and detractors from very close quarters, but I did not give in to them. I just kept playing along, taking small circumspect steps each day, keeping the purpose and meaning in life right in the centre. I did not want to die with my music still in me. I also did not want to commit the crime of not appreciating and harnessing the gift given to me by the creator. We all have a purpose in life, and we all need to enjoy it by making ourselves ready to make it our mainstream living. This is the only way to thrive joyfully, where obstacles will not bog you down but will give you a reason to keep going.

My transformation was not immediate. I meditated daily and looked at my debris of emotions, negative thoughts, and distractions. Also, I looked non-judgementally at those detractors or events, which sometimes held me back. I kept marching ahead by trusting innate and cosmic intelligence, which helped me unlearn stuff that did not serve me anymore.

That is when I became joyful and continued being so. This time, the 'achievements' were in line with my true identity; therefore, I wasn't addicted to it. Instead, those 'achievements' became a by-product of my joyful life and were no more the focus of my innately driven career. If you wish to be joyful, do not stop listening to the drummer inside you.

It is not by chance that you have chosen to read or listen to this book. You were conscious of making a shift in your life, and this book somehow appeared, among many others. Moments of serendipity keep happening in our lives, but we do not understand them and interpret those moments as 'life-as-usual'. Now that you are willing to uplift and empower your life, you need to do it by moving to a new level of consciousness. You must be very clear about what you are doing, how you are thinking, how you are feeling, how you are living, and overall, how you are being. Another thing you need to do is tell yourself now that this version of yours is not the real you and that you want to stop being that immediately. And this feeling of shifting from the unreal to the real must give you goose bumps.

What you are learning in this book is what I did and the steps I took in making changes. I believe that you may have done something similar in your life already, and you probably want to take it to the next level. The Soul In Harmony Conscious Leadership Framework I share in this book has also helped thousands of individuals across ten nationalities over ten years to unleash their true potential and have a holistic and fulfilling life – with true success, lasting happiness, and inner peace.

Very Important Disclaimer

My essence I had did not match my corporate career for the kind of person I was. Therefore, I was unfulfilled in continuing my old career trajectory. **I am not recommending that you quit your corporate career!**

In the next chapter, the most crucial one is where I will give you the details of how once you have shifted your consciousness to a higher level, you can create purpose and meaning in your life and live with a life vision. So, let us get to it.

❑

Conscious Leadership
Stage Five
Unified and Purposeful Growth

"You have to grow from the inside out. None can teach you, none can make you spiritual. There is no other teacher but your own soul."

– Swami Vivekananda

"Everything comes to us that belongs to us if we create the capacity to receive it."

– Rabindranath Tagore

"Those who have a 'why' to live can bear with almost any 'how'."

— Viktor E. Frankl, Man's Search for Meaning

"If you can tune into your purpose and align with it, setting goals so that your vision is an expression of that purpose, then life flows much more easily."

– Jack Canfield

"Musicians must make music; artists must paint; poets must write if they are ultimately at peace with themselves. What humans can be, they must be."

– Abraham Maslow

Craft Your Life Vision from Your Purpose

Who looks outside, dreams; who looks inside, awakens.

The heart of human excellence often begins to beat when you discover a purpose that grips yet frees you, challenges yet thrills you, and finally gives you a sense of meaning, passion, and fulfilment.

I genuinely believe that champions are not made in gyms. Champions are made from something deep inside them – a burning desire and a vision.

We can set our sights on the future by moving out of the past. One of my most memorable quotes by Thomas Carlyle that my English teacher used to say was – "The person without a purpose is like a ship without a rudder." During my quest period that I referred to in the previous chapter, I often came across Rumi's quote: "Everyone has been made for some particular work, and the desire for that work has been put in every heart."

When I was working on expanding my horizon to spread the message of what I have learned, I came across this quote from the passionately driven man, Steve Jobs, "If you are working on something exciting that you care about, you don't have to be pushed. The vision pulls you."

With my long experience of personal growth hacking, initiated at the young age of ten, I have realized that fulfilment comes only with living for a purpose. It is not enough to have lived. Winston Churchill said, "We should be determined to live for something." Out of the three decades of my quest, I struggled with the first two though I was making progress. The reason was that it took time for me to discover the purpose of life. But once this happened, the rest of the things aligned by themselves, and even the dots connected for the events in the past. During the quest, I realized we need to connect with our deeper selves to figure out our purpose. Your vision will become clear only when you look into your heart. In the next chapter, I will share a real-life story that deeply impacted me and how it steered my life. As I said, all the dots connect, provided we allow that to happen instead of forcing ourselves into directions we are unsure about.

A Real-Life Story That Impacted Me

Dr. Viktor Frankl, the author of the world-famous book *Man's Search for Meaning*, was a man who lived through an experience that is hard to imagine for a person in today's world. For almost four years, he lived in four different Nazi concentration camps, herded around, surviving on meagre rations of food and not knowing whether he would live to see the next day. Almost all his family members, including his wife, mother, father, and brother, suffered in the concentration camp due to their atrocities, and they all died in worse conditions inside the camp.

Yet the young Viktor survived due to his enormous willpower and courage to make it through this day, the next day that would come, and the next, all the way till his liberation came. He could do that because he found meaning in his life experiences and a sense of purpose that willed him to survive.

He lived through that traumatic experience to share with others how to live a better life despite any odds. Dr. Frankl suffered and lived through the ordeal only to be able to inspire and guide people to live through hardships and yet create a mark for themselves.

As a psychiatrist, he developed a logotherapy method to treat patients who suffered from depression, substance abuse, anxiety, and other problems. Logotherapy is a therapy based on helping you find your meaning and purpose in life so you can overcome any hardship.

After six years of Life Coaching practice, one of my clients pointed out that my style was similar to Dr. Viktor Frankl's logotherapy. Till then, I knew Dr. Frankl's story but did not know about his logotherapy.

Finding a 'Why' to Live

"Those who have a 'why' to live can bear with almost any 'how'." That is what Dr. Frankl finally inferred from his life situation. All that he meant was that we must have a purpose in life, and that purpose would help us find the unique path to our fulfilment. We will finally unlock fulfilment despite the challenges on that path.

Do not focus on what you want to be; focus on who you want to become. Define a purpose in life that becomes like the lighthouse in the ocean of life. You may also want to look at life's purpose as a compass in your hand that guides you in the direction as you progress on your unique life path. It keeps you centred, focused, and clear on what matters to you and what you want from life.

Here is the truth: You already know what your life purpose is!

The answer is waiting inside you. You just need to know how to pull it out. Once you know your purpose, the life vision unfolds!

The efforts and sacrifices required to unfold the purpose of life are well worth it. We transform as a person through the process of finding our life purpose. What follows is even more magical.

How Do You Create Your Life Vision?

An individual's life vision consists of three elements. You need to reflect consciously on the following:

1. List the **experiences you wish to have** (be passionate and creative while listing)

2. Reflect on the **areas of growth you want to create** in life (be optimistic and bold while listing)

3. **Contributions you want to make** to the world while doing the above two (be generous and purposeful while listing this)

When you combine these three elements, you have your life's vision for a purposeful life.

One needs to have self-awareness to sense the purpose of life. People often ask – what is the purpose of our life? I give a simplistic response to this. Living a life of purpose is our life's purpose at a high level – that is why the element of contribution is vital while creating your life vision. Ensure that the areas of growth and life experiences have something to contribute to this planet at some level.

How Does Having a Life Purpose Help?

The actual benefit of living a purposeful life is visible when challenging incidents happen and we are caught up in the cross-firing of life. Life vision comes to our rescue because it clarifies what to choose and what to let go of. We filter out what is urgent, important, or not so important. And then, it gives us the energy to persevere in that chosen path congruent with us and imperative for our fulfilment.

Just because life's purpose is deeply embedded inside us, it connects with our inner core values. As a result, when we make the right decisions based on our life purpose, we eliminate unwanted distractions and bring something fresh and unique into this world through our creation. It provides us with fulfilment – a life of true harmony!

Connect Life Vision with Gifts, Passion, and Values

Some people feel guilty about following their life purpose because they worry that it sounds like a selfish pursuit. However, our true purpose is to find our purpose. You need to recognize your gifts and use them to contribute uniquely to the world. It does not matter whether those gifts are about crafting a world-class corporation that will solve a significant problem in society, playing beautiful music for others to enjoy, doing a job that fulfils your soul, or simply bringing more joy to those around you.

When your original purpose becomes clear, you will be able to create a life vision and contribute to the world through that life vision.

What is G + P + V?

According to the author of the bestselling book, *Repacking Your Bags*, Richard Leider, the formula helps people decide on the next phase in their work life.

The equation for life purpose is, $G + P + V = P$.

(Gifts + Passions + Values = Purpose)

The 'Purpose' is nothing but your calling.

- **Gifts** prompt you to consider your strengths. It is always advisable to start with what you are good at.

- **Passion** is essentially asking what you care about. Are there issues or communities in the world that you are drawn towards more than anything else?

- **Values** are what drives your life like an engine. What is your non-negotiable lifestyle or personality to your work and life?

According to Leider, using your gifts toward something you are invested in and in an environment that suits your values will lead you to your calling. Unless you consider all three, you might be unhappy with your career choice.

What Life Purpose Feels Like

Finding your purpose feels a lot like finding yourself. You get to know who you are, what you are meant to do, and that you are unstoppable. You might suddenly not need others' validation because you are doing something so vital to yourself that no one could convince you otherwise. And pursuing your purpose is more of a journey than a destination.

Living your purpose feels like walking a path that is rightfully yours. So, you might have to step off the regular path you are currently on. You might need to carve your unique path ahead and feel strongly that you can do that. That is why pursuing your life purpose can be scary. Others may doubt you; at times, even you might doubt yourself. But somewhere deep inside, you resonate with this purpose.

Why is Life's Purpose Important?

If you do not strive or attempt to find your life purpose, then you are consciously signing up for a mediocre life, and I know you are not one among those. Bronnie Ware is an Australian nurse who spent several years in palliative care, caring for chronic patients in their last twelve weeks. She recorded their dying epiphanies in a blog, which gathered so much attention that she put her observations into a book called *The Top Five Regrets of the Dying*.

Do you know what the number one regret of terminally ill patients was?

"I wish I had the courage to live a life true to myself, not the life others expected of me."

Life purpose is not just important for a successful life. It helps to design a sustainable life with mental, emotional, and material well-being. I will explain this in the next chapter.

Impact of Life Purpose – Mental, Emotional and Material Well-Being

Research shows that finding your purpose is linked to living longer. Researchers surveyed nearly 7,000 older adults on the relationship between mortality and finding your purpose. Participants who did not have a strong sense of purpose were more than twice as likely to die prematurely as those who had figured out their purpose in life. Having a sense of purpose also reduces the incidence of cardiovascular events.

These results were universal, even when controlled for parameters such as income, race, gender, and education level. Researchers concluded that finding your purpose helps you live longer and is integral for happiness and fulfilment.

When you genuinely know your purpose, you will experience a sense of clarity like never before, as you can connect what you want to achieve to your ultimate fulfilment. You will feel passionate, driven, and laser-focused. You will stop flipping between the past and the future and start living in the present – which is the greatest gift you can give yourself.

A 2016 study published in the *Journal of Research and Personality* found that individuals who feel a sense of purpose are wealthier in life than those who think their work lacks meaning.

Therefore, the good news is that you do not have to choose between having wealth and living a meaningful life. You might discover that the more purpose you have, the more wealth you will make.

With all those benefits, it is clear that finding purpose and meaning in your life is essential. But purpose and meaning are not something that can be determined quickly.

The process requires plenty of self-awareness, self-reflection, letting go, and replacing damaging programs. These steps can help you reveal or find your purpose to begin living a more meaningful life.

I have already covered these topics for you to create a life of purpose.

Two Things that Keep You from Finding Your Purpose

Tony Robbins, the reputed motivational speaker and transformational coach, says, "If you're not growing, you're dying," which is why growth is intrinsically addictive to many of us. We naturally only feel fulfilled when we are improving ourselves in some way. Everything in life invites us to grow. We start feeling pain, fear, guilt, and anxiety when we stop growing. Then we fall prey to envy as we look around and see what others have that we do not. Instead of asking, 'What is my purpose in life', we are distracted and start craving status, material goods, and power. But all those things will ultimately be successful in creating a sense of emptiness inside you.

Progress and growth lead to happiness. So, if you ask yourself, "What is my purpose?" what you are asking for is progress, growth, and relevance – a true sense of fulfilment. And fulfilment is not a luxury or leisure activity but a necessity for a joyful soul.

You might believe that there are things that prevent people from finding their true purpose. They are comfortable where they are and do not want to rock the boat. The truth is that only two things prevent you from living a purposeful life.

1. **Comfort zone:** We as humans, long for stability and predictability, and our parasympathetic nervous system is also designed to switch to rest and digest mode intermittently. Staying in our comfort zones can keep us feeling safe and secure both emotionally and physically. But the downside is that over a prolonged period, this very 'comfort zone' starts haunting us and creates a false positive trap to prevent further growth. It keeps us imprisoned in unfulfilled careers

and unhealthy relationships. It prevents us from becoming who we are internally capable of being.

2. **Limiting beliefs:** I believe that our circumstances do not define our life; life is determined by the stories we tell ourselves about those circumstances. The stories we tell ourselves about who we are, can either restrict us to misery or catapult us towards fulfilment. Limiting beliefs such as, 'I am not good enough' and 'I do not deserve to be happy' leads to limiting attitudes and behaviours like fear of failure and self-sabotage. With wrong behaviours, we often end up developing bad habits and making wrong choices. Believing that we have no limitations and that even the sky is not a limit gives us the confidence to blossom in life and find our unique purpose. We can change our lives. We can do, have, and be exactly what we wish. Believe this and the life purpose will unfold.

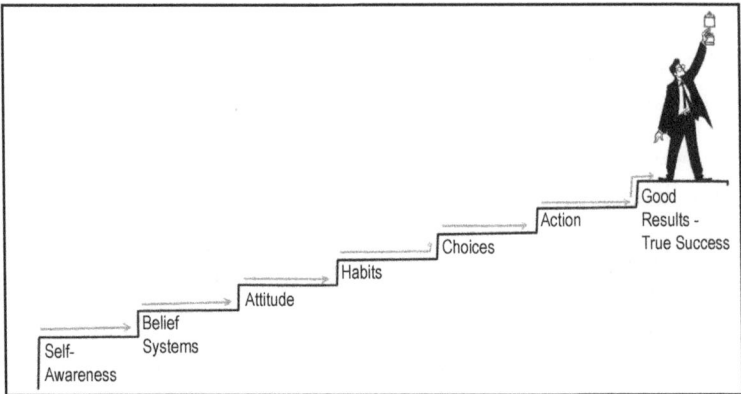

Fig. 7.1: **How Self-awareness Creates Results & Success**
Self-awareness is the foundation for achieving true success in life. When we cultivate our self-awareness, it works on a moment-to-moment basis and helps to rewrite our belief systems, attitudes, and habits leading to a mindful choice and action to achieve true success.

Follow this Lifestyle to Find Purpose in Life

A successful career, an affectionate family, a solid social network, and a good bank balance may seem like a perfect life. However, even those who can check each of these boxes might feel a sense of emptiness somewhere deep inside—and that "sense of emptiness" is due to their missing purpose in life.

"Finding your purpose" is more than just a cliché or a utopian dream. It is a tool for a better, happier, healthier, and, most importantly, fulfilling life that a few people consciously attempt to choose.

According to one analysis of the subject in *The New York Times*, only 25 per cent of American adults cite having a clear sense of purpose about what makes their lives meaningful, while 40 per cent either claim neutrality or say they do not.

Look inside yourself: Permit yourself to go deeper. Reflect on what drives you and what energizes you. What do you love to do? What do you care about so deeply that it motivates you to be in a state of striving or attempting to become better in that area? Now, how can you turn your passion and skills into something meaningful and constructive?

Be in a contribution mode: We can live life broadly in two different mindsets.

- What is in it for me?

- What can I contribute?

When we live with the second mindset, we can think of contributing through money, time, or talent. Whatever you do for a living, you can look at the work as your creation and approach

157

it from the standpoint of creating a masterpiece. It does not matter if you are a salesperson, an architect, a business leader, or an entrepreneur. Once you start approaching your work as a masterpiece, which is a work-in-progress, you will unknowingly begin to resonate with nature, and that will help you find your purpose.

Listen to feedback: Sometimes, it could be challenging to pinpoint the things you feel passionate about. After all, you probably like to do many different things, and the things you love to do may have become so deep-rooted and automatic in your life that you do not realize how important those things are.

But here's the thing. The people close to you might be able to give you some insight or clues. There is a good chance you are already demonstrating your passion and purpose to those around you without even realizing it.

It would be a tremendous idea to reach out to people and ask what reminds them of you or what they think of when you enter their minds. Or, stay mindful when someone pays you a compliment. Write those observations down and look for patterns.

People might think of you as a kind and helpful person, a great entertainer, a good mentor, or a sharp entrepreneur with creative ideas. Hearing others say what they notice about you might reinforce some of the passions you have already been embodying.

Surround yourself with positive people: As they say, you are the average of those five people you spend the most time with. While counting the above, do not consider your co-workers or family members you feel obliged to see. Think about the people you consciously and willingly choose to spend time with outside your workplace and family functions.

The people you surround yourself with say something about you. You will draw inspiration if you are surrounded by people making positive changes.

On the other hand, if the people around you are negative-minded folks, they will drag you down. It is an uphill task to feel passionate and purposeful when surrounded by people not interested in making positive contributions to their life.

Be open to meeting new people: It is easy to scroll through social media when you are alone or waiting for someone or have less load at your work. Resist that urge and attempt to start conversations and meet new people.

Even though striking up conversations with strangers may feel awkward initially, talking to a broad group of people outside your immediate social circle can open your eyes to activities, causes, or career opportunities that you never even knew existed. You might discover new activities to explore or different places to visit. And those activities might be vital to helping you find your purpose.

Explore your interests: Is there a topic you are always talking about or have deep emotions about, or is there an idea or point of view you want to spread? Do you regularly share articles about the environment, self-development, start-up ideas, and so on?

Are your pictures and videos on Instagram talking about your passion for travel and history, or does it point towards your interests in gardening, meditation, and healthy living? Take a closer look at the conversations you enjoy most with people you meet face-to-face. Do you like talking about business or history? Or do you prefer sharing the latest self-help or money-saving tips you discovered?

The things you like to talk about and enjoy sharing on social media may reveal the things that give you purpose in life. The good news is that you are already embodying it to some extent.

Consider injustices that bother you or major transformations you would like to bring: Many people have their favourite causes or passion projects surrounding injustice in the world. Is there anything that keeps you awake at night, or you might have researched some topic extensively, or something that bothers you to the core? (Note: this injustice can lead you to core values).

It might be about mastering yourself despite distractions in today's world, employee well-being in a demanding business environment, holistic health amid a rat race, parenting post-pandemic for Gen Z, animal welfare, or childhood obesity. Perhaps the idea of senior citizens spending the holidays alone makes you emotional and urges you to do something about it.

You do not necessarily have to engage in your purpose full-time. You might find that your career allows you to afford to help a cause you feel passionate about. Or, you might find that you can donate time—as opposed to money—to give to a reason you believe in.

Discover what you love to do: This tip is simplistic. Unlike the above advice, simply engaging your thoughts on what you genuinely love doing can also help you find your purpose.

Do you love health and well-being? Your skills might be best used to create advocacy for a healthy lifestyle that can shield the stressed-out individuals trapped in a competition they cannot exit.

Do you love painting? If yes, check if playing with colours add new zest to your life. In this case, you might want to immerse yourself in the artist community and find out how you can share your masterpiece with the world.

Consider what skills, talents, and passions you bring to the table. Then, brainstorm how you might turn your passion into something meaningful to you.

Express yourself: This advice is related to the above point but is more about expressing openly. Sometimes creative outlets and other forms of self-expression (e.g., writing, painting, drawing, playing music, mindful meditation) can help you gain a sense of purpose. Or, you might decide to experience different cultures and sights through travel. Do whatever inspires you and which enables you to express your inner self.

Make connections: A sense of purpose often grows from having meaningful connections with others and realizing that you are part of something larger than yourself. This helps to build and keep the momentum in whatever you have been striving for. This community of like-minded tribes enables you to lift yourself back up if you falter on this journey. Look at the people around you in your community. What do you have in common with them? Can you join them?

Let me explain this. Finding your life purpose does not happen overnight. It is a quest. Sometimes you will get caught up in daily pressures, but do not let yourself lose sight of the things that are worthwhile to you. You are here for a reason. Part of your journey is finding out what that reason is. Once you find your purpose, you will agree it was well worth the effort. Your life will then have a meaning, you will be able to stand for something, and in people's minds, your name will be synonymous with something bigger than you – that's the legacy you can leave behind, my friend.

How Can Leaders Help Employees Find Purpose in their Work?

Organizations cannot expect leaders to help their employees find purpose in their work by sharing a mission statement. They must help their people connect their passion, core values, and strengths to their daily work. Essentially, it is all about joining the dots between 'who you are inside', 'what you do' and 'how you do it'.

This lets employees connect with their deeper selves. This approach can bring fulfilment that can light up their lives with positivity and enthusiasm. This will ultimately lead to a vibrant workplace for everyone to find their sweet spot through their work. The work does not stay a separate entity; it becomes an extension of your identity for good. As a result, the stress at work sublimes by itself.

According to a recent Gallup poll, Gen Z and millennials (who make up nearly half of the full-time workforce in the US) value 'belonging to a company with a solid moral compass.' They appreciate ethical leadership and want to know that their work has a purpose that connects with theirs and positively influences the world.

A Deloitte study revealed in 2016 that people feel loyal to companies that support their career and life ambitions. Irrespective of level, career, or industry, our innate nature needs to find a personal sense of meaning in what we do.

Leaders can create an environment where workers can connect their inner sense of purpose with what matters in their work with a simple conversation.

Organizations spend considerable time and resources on corporate values and mission statements. However, even the most inspiring of those, from Tesla's "world's transition to sustainable energy" to Google's "organize the world's information" and

Microsoft's "empower every person and every organization on the planet" — tend to recede to the background during the daily grind of an exhausting working day.

Method to Align Individual Purpose to Work Profile and Organization

The standard check-in method involves Five Areas of Inquiry (FAI) and is a way to help employees explore and figure out their inner purpose and link it to their work.

Leaders can ask their employees the following questions:

What are you good at doing?

- Which work activities require less effort for you?

- What do you tend to volunteer for because you believe you are the ideal person to do it?

- What have you been noticed for throughout your career, which was very distinct?

The idea here is to help people identify their strengths and open up possibilities.

What do you enjoy?

- In a typical workweek, what do you look forward to doing often?

- What on your calendar or a to-do list energizes you?

- How would you spend your time if you could design your job without restrictions?

These questions help people find or rediscover what they love about work.

What feels most useful?

- Which kind of results or work outcomes make you most proud and inspired?

- Which of your tasks are most critical to the team or organization?

- What are your life's core values, and how does your work align with them?

This line of inquiry highlights the inherent value of a particular work.

What creates a sense of forward fortification?

- What are you learning here today that you will use in the future somewhere someday?

- What do you envision for yourself in your next phase of life?

- How is your work getting you closer to what you want for yourself in your next life phase?

The goal is to show how today's work helps them advance towards future goals.

How do you relate to others?

- Which working partnerships, associations, or collaborations are best suited for you?

- What would the office of your favourite team member look like?

- How does your work enrich your family and social connections?

These questions encourage people to think about and foster relationships that make work more meaningful.

It is challenging to guide the employees towards purpose and align them with the organization's objective. These inquiry method guidelines can help in doing that.

Create a Purpose-Driven Organization for Corporate Excellence

During the recruitment process, it is an individual's responsibility to self-reflect and delve into the meaning and purpose of life and check if this aligns with the corporate values and objectives. This reduces the unwanted friction that could cause attrition resulting in the corporation's lost time, money and talent.

Sense of Purpose and a Sense of Impact

The mature corporations have a due diligence mechanism in their recruitment process that will also check if the candidate is deriving a sense of purpose and a sense of impact both from the job one has applied for.

Two examples of a misaligned sense of purpose and a sense of impact are as follows:

1. An artist as an art gallery employee – She loves painting but does not like sales – this passionate artist's sense of purpose for this work is high, but her sense of impact for the same work is not ample. This is a misfit!

   Solution: Sales training for this art gallery employee will add a sense of impact to her because she can also leverage this new skill for her own life.

2. A sales performer in a top corporate who does not enjoy sales performs well at his job because he might have natural sales skills or he stretches himself. Therefore, this sales professional has a good sense of impact. But deep inside, he does not love sales activities. That is why he lacks a sense of purpose despite having a high sense of impact. Eventually, he gets burnt out. He takes frequent leaves and is unfulfilled

168

even in his personal and social life despite the outer 'success and achievements.' This is also a misfit.

Solution: If HR and the Sales Specialist's manager can help align his sense of purpose to a suitable role inside the organization or check if things have shifted in his personal life. It would be even better if HR could institutionalize self-reflection for candidates even before they apply for the jobs. This is where the candidates can check their company objectives and job's key results with their life purpose and core values.

Only when there is a sense of purpose and sense of impact for an individual in a particular career is there a psychological safety net that weaves by itself. The talent gets further empowered, leading to healthy team culture and corporate excellence.

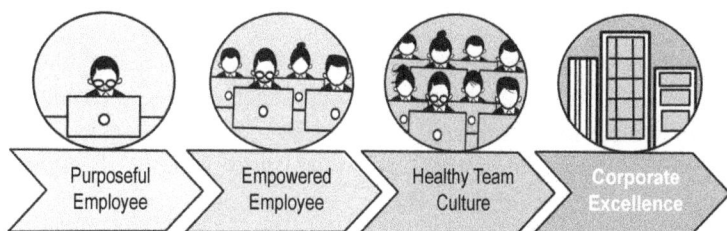

Fig. 7.2: **Purposeful Employee is the Foundation of Corporate Excellence**
A purposeful employee is a self-aware and empowered employee. These employees create a healthy team culture. This healthy team culture results in corporate excellence, where every employee is highly engaged and inspired.

A corporation creates a vision and mission statement. It lays down the values to align employees and keep them congruent with the organization's ethos. After that, the Objectives and Key Results (OKR) are derived from the values.

- Have you thought about how this would help in curbing the rising attrition?

- Have you wondered how the vision, mission, values, and OKRs be linked to all the recruits' (C-Suites and rank-and-file) life purpose to create a cohesive team?

169

Well, this is possible! That is why Google initiates its recruitment process and asks the candidates to go into self-reflection before applying for the coveted job. (Refer to the Self-reflection section of the book).

Struggling with Talent Crisis

Aligning employees' purpose to corporate values is vital to addressing the deepening 'talent crisis'. Those organizations (for example, Google) with a recruitment process that ascertains the candidate's purpose alignment with the corporate values and objectives do very well in curbing the attrition rate plaguing the industry and addressing the talent crunch head-on. Beyond the talent crunch, the 'individual purpose – corporate values' fitment leads to healthy and cohesive corporate culture.

Many corporations, when faced with business challenges such as dipping revenue, declining bottom line, eroding shareholders' value, losing market share, and shabby customer service, the corporations become clueless as to what is happening. To shake things up, the leaders of these organizations start providing training, altering incentives, and micromanaging projects with disappointing results.

These approaches do not work out because they are reactive towards people. The wrongful methods are to be blamed and not the people.

That is a hard truth to accept. If, like many executives, you are applying conventional economic logic, you, as a leader, view your employees as 'Resources' (and not human beings with talent and purpose) and design your organizational practices and culture tightly to arrest the economic leakage that does not pay off as you had hoped. The employees' talents, gifts, and purpose need to be harnessed to formulate a solid partnership with them for a 360-degree, long term and multi-dimensional growth of both people and the corporation.

So, you are faced with two options:

- Double down on that tightening approach on the assumption that you need more or stricter controls to achieve the desired business objectives.

- You can align the organization with an authentic higher purpose that supports your business interests and helps guide your decisions.

If you succeed in doing the latter, your people will try new things, move into deep learning, align their purpose with that of organizations, and make surprising contributions in a heart-centred environment.

Most organizations embrace purpose when they are faced with a crisis. This situation forces the leaders to challenge their assumptions about motivation and performance and experiment with new approaches. But you do not need to wait for a dreadful crisis to hit before you embrace a purpose-driven approach to corporate excellence.

In the next part, I will explain how corporations can build purpose-driven organizations.

Build a Purpose-Driven Organization before the Chips are Down

Do not wait for things to go south to take the appropriate action to retain the talent. Instead, organizations can have a proactive approach to attracting, hiring, and retaining talent. We have discussed a few methods earlier.

The guidelines below will help you build a purpose-driven organization even before your business starts to suffer. Following seven key steps enables you to overcome the most significant barrier to embracing purpose—the short-term "transactional" view of employee motivation.

1. **Have an inspired workforce:** According to economists, every employer faces the "principal-agent problem," which is the standard model for describing an organization's relationships with its workers. Let me explain: The principal (the employer) and the agent (the employee) form a work contract. The agent is effort averse. An employee will deliver a certain amount of work for a specific salary. Since effort is costly, the agent underperforms in providing it unless the principal offers incentives to counter that tendency.

   This model prohibits the notion of a fully engaged workforce. If you can find one good example—a person or a team that exceeds the norms, you can inspire other employees. Look for more excellence, examine the purpose that drives the excellence, and then imagine it permeating into your entire workforce.

2. **Discover the purpose:** Remember, you do not invent a higher purpose; it already exists. You can discover it through compassion—by feeling and understanding the deepest everyday needs of your workforce. That involves asking stimulating questions, listening and reflecting. An

organization often discovers its purpose when they are faced with a challenge.

3. **Embrace authenticity:** Leaders must identify a purpose and a set of values and live them with integrity. Be authentic in doing business with profit and customer satisfaction in mind and treat employees as valued human beings, not just human resources. If your purpose is genuine, people understand that because it drives every decision, and you do things other companies would not.

4. **Stimulate individual learning:** As leaders embrace a higher purpose, they recognize that learning and development are powerful incentives. Employees are inherently inclined to think, learn, and grow.

5. **Turn mid-level managers into purpose-driven leaders:** To build an inspired, committed, and stimulated workforce, you will need middle managers who know the organization's purpose, deeply connect with it, and lead with their moral strength. This is where many companies fall short and mid-level managers cannot embody the organization's purpose. As a result, the frontline workers see through this and become disengaged.

6. **Connect the people to the purpose:** Once leaders at the top and mid-level have internalized the organization's purpose, they must help their subordinates align it with their day-to-day tasks. But an out-and-out top-down mandate does not work smoothly. The employees need to help drive this process because the purpose is more likely to influence the culture and behaviour, even when managers are not watching how people handle things. This is where conscious self-leadership takes shape.

7. **Unleash the positive energizers:** Every organization has a pool of change agents whose latent talent goes untapped. This pool is a network of positive energizers.

Remember that these self-aware change agents influence the organization's culture; then, the culture impacts the performance and brings excellence. The culture is not created by discovering the corporation's purpose but by letting these catalysts' self-awareness soar to a level where they sprinkle the purpose with raw authenticity. They naturally inspire others with their drive. Their high self-awareness quotient makes them open and willing to take the initiative. Once the key energizers are enlisted, they can play a pivotal role in every step of the organizational cultural change. These people are easy to identify, and the best part is that others also trust them.

❏

RE-BORN
(The Original You)

RE-BORN
(The Original You)

Becoming the Original You is Now Possible

Earlier in this book, I told you that you do not have to create a purpose but search for it. It lies deep inside and is very safe. You might ask, 'If my purpose is a part of me and it is within me, then what is the striving all about?

The good news is – that you are correct in asserting that the purpose is a part of you. One interesting thing to note here is that we have separated ourselves so much from the natural person that we are and we need to try to meet that original person and then unite as one forever. We have allowed the environmental influences involuntarily from the womb to where we stand now. The external forces acted like distractions, and we kept piling each layer after layer. And the reality today is that most of us have started believing that the conditioned identity is the real identity. My friend, you are unique! Unique because, somewhere deep inside, you still have a feeling, and you know it, though faintly, that you have an identity that is much more powerful and unblemished, and that is the belief and hope with which you had chosen to read or listen to this book.

I will help you practise this 'Soul In Harmony Conscious Leadership Framework' in real life. Stay with me till the end. We are not done yet. The whole book is designed so that I am taking you step by step on this Conscious Leadership journey. You have read till here; now is the time to bring it together.

You are your accountability partner as you go through this journey of unravelling your purpose. For this, you must raise your consciousness to tap into that space of silence and stillness inside you where your purpose is safely placed. We, as a human race, are meant not to stop growing. We all yearn for progress, and that leads to reinvention.

Reinvention is what you will do by implementing the Conscious Leadership Framework. Reinvention is different from achievement. Seeking an achievement usually implies an 'end.' You win the trophy, and then you are 'done.' As soon as you are 'done,' you are no longer on the journey, which means you stop growing.

That is not true in the case of reinvention. Reinvention, however, leaves the end open—which is a good thing. Reinvention is what allows you endless opportunities to continue exploring new parts of yourself. Exploration is a growth journey, and growth, in this sense, will start when you are inward-facing. The growth will manifest outwardly as an individual, team, family, organization and society.

Whenever you find something about yourself you want to change, you need to harness your self-awareness, put in concerted self-reflection, accept the constraints and blocks, look into the negative programming to remove them, and then build a life vision true to yourself. This is the way to reinvent yourself.

178

Tapping into the 'Original You'

You will use the first four of the five steps of the 'Soul In Harmony Conscious Leadership Framework' to balance your mind. The fifth and final step of this framework is about unified growth through finding your purpose and meaning in life with a heart-centred approach. This helps you create a perfect life vision that will unfold the 'original you' by nurturing that potent seed lying inside, just waiting to sprout out someday. The seed contains all the right ingredients for who you are naturally. How do you truly get the 'original you' to sprout out?

Your daily practices, such as mindfulness, meditation, journaling, introspection, and alpha affirmation for manifestation, will be vital. Reading inspirational books that resonate with you is like tending to that potent seed waiting to burst through the earth's womb during this time. By doing this, you will create your armour for a brighter tomorrow.

As you imagine your future where the 'original you' seed is about to manifest, it is time to prepare and ensure the potential tree grows well and bears fruits. The preparations are similar to creating a safety fence protecting your vulnerable potential from adverse environmental conditions. The armour for you will be the intensity with which you will fall in love with the process of becoming the 'original you'. This intense feeling of love is a higher frequency emotion on Hawkin's Consciousness Scale and acts as a fertile ground to manifest the future tree and fruits you have envisioned. You will no longer be in survival mode but will thrive on making way for the 'original you'.

Playing the 'Original You'

Once you have tapped into your original avatar, the next thing you must do is play that embodiment repeatedly till you become acquainted with that original version of yours. From a neuroscientific perspective, the more you fire those neurological circuits together, the more strongly you wire that circuit.

Neuroscientists say, **'the neurons that fire together, wire together.'**

And if you continuously and consciously generate a series of thoughts based on your 'Original You' avatar, the mind will naturally shift to that original level, and you do not have to try too hard after some time.

As a result, when you repeat the same mental frame consciously and repeatedly, playing the 'Original You' over a long period, it will become natural, familiar, automatic, and subconscious. You will then begin to recognize and remember the 'Original You' that you were meant to be with the unique superpower, gifts, and talents you had forgotten in your childhood.

❏

Afterword
If You Follow Your Purpose, Others Will Follow You

One of the biggest lies is that we can live a fulfilling and joyful life without knowing the meaning of our life. Neither did our schools teach us nor did our elders emphasize the importance of purpose and meaning. We cannot ignore the life purpose element in the life equation for joy and harmony. If we do so, we suffer in mid-life and wonder about the emptiness deep inside. The situation is tricky because satisfaction is missing despite having a decent job, active business, happy marriage, caring relationships, and robust health. We realize that we did not make any impact on this planet. We follow the eat-work-sleep cycle; that is all! One fine day, something happens, and we face the stark reality and ask ourselves – "What about our dreams, passion, and purpose? It could be a health breakdown, a job loss, a significant loss in business, a breakup, or a divorce. We are too late to ask ourselves, "Did we make any difference to this planet?"

We must become conscious self-leaders before we hit a point of no return! That means we must turn inwards and discover who we are and what we are meant for.

When we become self-aware, we get a handle to create an identity shift. This shift produces meaningful results in our lives. Because all individuals are unique, our journey from self-awareness to Unified & Purposeful Growth must be distinctive.

When we, as conscious leaders, align to our purpose, our vibes re-orient and allow us to make appropriate choices to get intentional results from our life. We become perfectly natural beings and genuinely harmonious. To reach this state, we must display discipline, consistency, and self-awareness as fundamental values.

Apart from the above values, we as parents must instil a few values critical to our children and can serve them a lifetime, no matter what they become.

I remember my father used this proverb – "**Time and tide wait for no man**" while explaining the importance of time and how we must value it. Time is more valuable than money, and I try my best not to while it away or waste it. I am always punctual. I never went to school late, even a single day, nor did I arrive late for any meeting ever.

My father often used two more quotations: "**Fortune favours the brave**" and "**God helps those who help themselves.**" This is so clearly etched in my psyche that I will give all the credit to my father for nurturing my self-belief and risk-taking ability. That is the prime reason I make big decisions and try new things to experience the best life I can live with my gifts and talents.

My story of how I came out from my stammering habit by deciding to go on the stage to kill fear, how I chose to redefine myself after fifteen years of corporate career and launch a human transformation business suggests how deeply these values created brain tattoos that permitted me 'to take the risk.' In most of my retreats and workshops, participants often ask me, "How did you dare to take up those risks?"

My answer to them is – "In fact, these risks were not a risk for me because once I became aware of who I was, there was no more doubt in mind; I had to walk that path. My self-talk was positive and conclusive."

To take my stammering issue head-on, the self-talk was – *If I want to impact the world, I cannot live with this hurdle lifelong.*

For moving on from a corporate career to launching a life transformation business, the self-talk was – *My mission is to help individuals become heart-centred, purpose-driven, and values-based leaders, I need to take a leap of faith.*

I did not compete with anyone in both these life struggles. I was only focused on improving myself to make a difference in others' lives. I somehow knew that one of my core values was to bring transformation to others. Later as I deep-dived into life, I discovered three others: freedom, authenticity, and personal growth.

You become unstoppable when you focus on transforming others using your core values. Imagine if, in both my above life situations, I had resisted my life condition, then I would have struggled to give up my stammering habit of negative self-talk – "I can't bear it anymore, why no one cares, how can I be like this, how pathetic is life," and so on. Even for the career shift, my negative self-talk would be – "Jobs don't make me happy anymore; I am doomed, and what else can I do?"

Today I have impacted thousands of individuals by helping them to tap into the hidden greatness deep in their hearts. This 'Soul In Harmony Conscious Leadership Framework' would not have been possible had I not gone through the churning in life that I went through.

Likewise, if you follow your purpose with unique core values, others will follow you.

It would help if you made unique choices and sacrifices on this Conscious Leadership quest while learning the lessons that come your way and having acceptance for things outside your control. I have also explained in detail how we must work on our mental conditioning and harmful programs that do not allow us to become the super powerful original ones. Self-awareness is an essential trait we must cultivate to reflect on our life and its purpose. Only after we develop self-awareness can we hack into self-reflection to create a distinct life vision with a sense entrenched in our hearts.

When we retune ourselves with life's unique purpose, we become ultra-powerful and contain an indomitable spirit to conquer whatever obstacles come our way.

For Corporates

Corporate excellence is possible with refined team culture, and this culture is possible only when we have conscious humans (they are not just resources).

The answer is – To cultivate self-awareness for purpose; there is no other path!

With a 'Soul In Harmony Conscious Leadership Framework,' the corporate scene will brim with creativity, productivity, and resilience. The result is corporate excellence.

The leaders emerging from this kind of culture will be purposeful leaders who connect with humans more profoundly and make the business environment profitable and sustainable.

❑

Cheat Sheet to Jumpstart Your Conscious Leadership

Twelve conscious leadership questions to ask yourself

1. What three words describe me the best?

2. What are my priorities for the next 12 months?

3. What are my most significant achievements in life so far?

4. What are my biggest failures/setbacks/challenges so far?

5. What kind of individuals do I want in my first circle?

6. What would I tell my 10-year-old self?

7. Who is/are my role model/s these days?

8. What makes me feel energized?

9. What do I need to let go to build forward momentum?

10. What brings me the most joy?

11. What would it be if I could share one message with the world?

12. What do I love the most about myself?

Five daily questions conscious leaders will ask themselves

1. How will I show up for today?

2. What do my people need and why?

3. Who will I thank/recognize/appreciate?

4. Who needs constructive feedback?

5. What conscious leadership attributes do I focus on today?

To become something you never were, you must do some things you never did.

Do it with a Purpose (why) and an Intention (aim).

Book Reviews

"I have always held a view that at all levels of leadership, the supervisor's role is not as much about supervising as about creating a superior vision. The vision encompasses a sense of accomplishment in attaining a higher purpose. Aligning the team to such a vision delivers amazing results. Sandiip provides the insights to align ourselves with a purposeful approach to growth thereby creating a powerful formula for success".
–Arvind Thakur - Former Vice Chairman and Managing Director, NIIT Technologies Ltd

Igniting Conscious Leadership is the way forward for both individuals and corporations. Self-awareness and insight are truly the first steps to a transformation of the modern workplace and personal fulfilment. Sandiip's methodology to re-sculpt a negative self-image is practical and doable. Sandiip brings in his personal narrative skillfuly and with great conviction even as he draws on current research on organizations and management practices. A simple and effective read!
– Geetanjali Pandit, Bestselling Author and Columnist, Transformational Speaker and Coach, Former CHRO *The India Today Group, The Indian Express Group* **and Zee Media Corporation.**

"I found the approach in the book very clear and transparent, and the fact that Sandiip has shared his own experiences should help readers connect ever more closely to the message. A book is written to inspire conscious leadership and self-awareness in every extraordinary human being - in every one of us. Take the leap of faith!"
– Aditya Purandare, Managing Director, Kraiburg TPE India

"How we show up as leaders is significantly influenced by our way of "being". This book makes for an immensely valuable and insightful read for anyone who would like to tap into their inner self to achieve purpose, meaning and success."
– Anil Jalali, Executive Coach, ex-CHRO - Capgemini India

"Reveals what it takes to lead with a purpose-driven agenda. It closely explores the vision, virtues, and mindset required for providing a roadmap for innovative, value-based leadership in all walks of life. The book provides strategies for the individual and the organization through a storytelling approach. Each chapter will enrich your wisdom culminating in an empowering call to action for all those who want to put people above everything else."
– Dr. Sriharsha A. Achar, CHRO, Star Health and Allied Insurance

"Thought-provoking and very well-structured book that will propel your journey towards self-actualization and help discover a more awake and aware leader in you".
– Animesh Kumar, Chief HR Officer, Novopay

"Extremely empowering and has the potential to resurrect a broken soul. It can help one rediscover their hidden but true power. Sandiip's 5-step conscious leadership framework focuses on how our relationship with ourselves is vital for achieving

'true success' that leads to organizational success. It serves as an authoritative guide for people who aspire to be or are already a leader by fixing the missing and crucial 'fulfilment' piece essential for a holistic picture!"

– Vipul Dave, Ex-Liberty Steel CHRO

"In my view, a key role of a leader is to work with several minds (team) and it can be done effectively only when the leader understands his/her mind better. That calls for conscious leadership with primary focus on self-awareness or self-reflection. Sandip has been a champion in this space and is enabling others to enhance leadership skills through his experiences and simple frameworks. A must read for people who aspire to become true leaders in this VUCA world."

–Venkatraman Umakanth - Vice President & Head - Analytics & IT | Animations, Vee Technologies Pvt. Ltd.

❏

Bibliography

Baer, R. A., Hopkins, J., Krietemeyer, J., and Toney, L. (2006). Using Self-Report Assessment Methods to Explore Facets of Mindfulness. SAGE Journals, 27-45.

Dondi, M., Klier, J., Panier, F., and Schubert, J. (2021). Defining the Skills Citizens Will Need in the Future World of Work. McKinsey, 2-22.

Elizabeth Scott, P. (2021, March 23). How to Find Satisfaction at Your Current Job.

Gallup. (2020). Gallup's Perspective on Employee Burnout: Causes and Cures. *Gallup. California: Gallup.*

Hedges, K. (2017). 5 Questions to Help Your Employees Find Their Inner Purpose. Harvard Business Review.

Jena, L. K., and Pradhan, S. (2018). Workplace Spirituality and Employee Commitment: The Role of Emotional Intelligence and Organisational Citizenship Behaviour in Indian Organisations. Journal of Enterprise Information Management, 21-58.

Khullar, D. (2018, January 1). Finding Purpose for a Good Life. But Also a Healthy One. The New York Times.

Kobau, R., Sniezek, J., Zack,, M. M., and Lucas, R. E. (2010). Well-Being Assessment: An Evaluation of Well-Being Scales for Public Health and Population Estimates of Well-Being Among US Adults. Applied Psychology: Health & Well-Being, 272-297.

McCraty, R., Atkinson, M., and Tomasino, D. (1993). MODULATION OF DNA CONFORMATION BY HEART-FOCUSED INTENTION. Proceedings of the Third Annual Conference of the International Society for the Study of Subtle Energy and Energy Medicine, Monterey, California, 58-62.

Musich, S., Wang, S. S., Kraemer, Sandra., and Hawkins, K. (2018). Purpose in Life and Positive Health Outcomes Among Older Adults. Population Health Management, 139-147.

Quinn, R. E., and Thakor, A. V. (2018). Creating a Purpose Driven Organization. Harvard Business Review, 78-85.

❑

Your Notes

Your Notes

Your Notes

Your Notes

CPSIA information can be obtained
at www.ICGtesting.com
Printed in the USA
LVHW030124090323
741211LV00032B/1418